Preface

Less than three years ago the personal computer was touted as the most important product since the invention of the automobile. Today, this estimate may be a gross understatement as computer technology finds its way into many more aspects of day to day living than was previously imagined. Most experts agree that because of the personal computer, we are on the threshold of a technological era so great that it will reshape the nature of human interaction on this planet for decades to come.

The personal computer responsible for this is a small typewriter to book-size device that you can purchase today for $200 to $5000. A consequence of tremendous advancements in solid-state technology, these "mind amplifiers" are getting smaller and smarter each year, and already some are able to actually speak several different languages! These remarkable new products are destined to become a personal-assistant-helper-tool for their lucky owners, that will help them with their business, including learning, selecting goods to buy, paying bills, playing games, providing directions, and so on.

This book is the first to explain what it would be like to own a computer—what you could do with it, how it would make your life easier, and how you might go about buying one and investigating it for your own uses. This book presents these devices as the simple and easy to control tools that they truly are.

The first chapter explains just what a personal computer is, where it came from, and an estimate of what the future holds for this rapidly changing technology. A detailed history of the personal computer market is presented. To make your understanding of computer concepts even clearer, a brief glossary of the most often encountered computer buzz words, complete with definitions and a practice sentence using the word is listed in Chapter 2. Chapter 3 illustrates some of the ways personal computers are being used today in applications to make life easier. Programming, which sets the computer apart from all other products, and makes it a chameleon-like multifunction machine, is covered in Chapter 4. The programming chapter has been expanded in this second edition to help the reader understand the new emphasis on computer software.

Next, Chapter 5 details the necessary "hardware" that makes up the personal computer, including input/output units, peripherals, microprocessors, buses, interfaces, memories, and many more. Because of the growing number of auxiliary products on the market that can be hooked up to a personal computer, this hardware section has been greatly expanded in this second edition of the book. Each topic is covered in a simple, easy to follow language and the most recent peripheral products available for your computer are explained.

For those persons serious about buying a personal computer, Chapter 6 presents details on 30 popular personal and small business computer products on the market today in terms of cost, capability, models, expansion, and so on. The final chapter tells you how to get started in this exciting field, whether you plan to use it for your home, hobby, or business. For readers who wish to get deeper into computer operations, an appendix on computer number systems is included.

This book has been especially designed to be your first investment in the personal computer field. It provides the newcomer with the knowledge and confidence to utilize this marvel of our time. In this new edition we bring you more information and several new sections to enhance your knowledge further of this exciting market. It is our hope that this book stimulates and helps you to utilize this marvelous technology in your own life.

MITCHELL WAITE
MICHAEL PARDEE

Acknowledgments

The authors would like to give a warm thank you to the following individuals who helped in the creation of this book.

Baker, Joy, Executive Assistant, Intelligent Systems Corp.

Barrick, Lora, Marketing Department, Exidy, Inc.

Bender, Janice Feldstein, Account Executive, Edelman Public Relations (for Mattel).

Billings, Michael, Owner, Computerland of Marin.

Bradford, Marian, Corporate Assistant, Vector Graphics, Inc.

Heber, Judy, Administrative Assistant, Cromemco.

Inafuku, Ray, Northwest District Sales Manager, Commodore Business Machines, Inc.

Kahn, Ted, Educational Consultant, Atari, Inc.

Lee, Pat, National Publicity and Promotion Manager, Tandy Corporation/Radio Shack.

Marchan, Lettie R., Marketing Communications Secretary, North Star Computers, Inc.

Roybal, Phil, Marketing Manager, Apple Computer Inc.

Ruddock, Steve, Product Publicity, Hewlett Packard.

Tauscher, Debbie, Marketing Services, Dynabyte, Inc.

Walker, Ellen, Marin Community Mental Health Center.

Wedel, Lynn, Marketing Services, Apple Computer, Inc.

Whitman, Lois, HWH Enterprises (for Sinclair Ltd.).

Contents

CHAPTER 1

Introduction

WHAT ARE PERSONAL COMPUTERS?

Personal computers are small computers that are inexpensive to own. They are the result of many recent developments in electronic technology. Personal computers can do everything that big computers can do, but in less space and for less money. They are in their infancy but will soon become a common appliance in the home.

WHERE DID THEY COME FROM?

Several years ago, the development of the transistor made possible many modern conveniences. The first product to become popular was the transistor radio, which was often nicknamed the "transistor." A few years later, transistors began appearing in all types of consumer products. Some television manufacturers were employing transistors in their sets to prolong the lives of their products. Stereo systems were also being manufactured using this new marvel of technology. Soon, every electronic device that once used vacuum tubes had been redesigned to utilize the transistor.

It was only natural that computers also would be converted to transistorized versions, since the early models which used vacuum tubes were very large and expensive. By the late 1950s almost all contemporary computers were using transistors. This phenomenon became known as "second generation" computers, since they had evolved from the old tube-style models.

The infamous transistor.

It was during this time that the "space race" was in full swing. The United States was in competition with the Soviet Union to be the first country to successfully launch an artificial satellite. This would inevitably lead to putting a man into space and finally on the moon. Since the "space-going" electronics had to be small and lightweight, the transistor was perfected to a fine state. The research that went into this perfection provided the groundwork for the mass production of "solid-state" electronic circuits. These new devices were called "integrated circuits" (ICs) because they were entire electronic circuits fabricated into a single package. Like the transistor, the IC was manufactured from semiconductor material but in such a way that not one, but many transistors could be produced on one tiny "chip." The implications of such a development are shocking! Electronic devices which once required many discrete parts could be built using only a few ICs. As the manufacturing expertise has improved, the "unit cost" of such IC devices continues to drop. In the early 1970s the first evidence of this technological revolution became known to the public in the form of the electronic calculator.

Courtesy NASA

The space race.

The first calculators were the direct result of the ability to design electronic devices using integrated circuits. The thousands of transistors necessary to make an electronic calculator work could now be contained within just a few IC chips. Although the first calculators were rather expensive ($300-$500), they were very low priced by comparison to what they would have cost just a few short years before. As the consumer market began to realize the value of owning an electronic calculator, the demand for them increased. This guarantee of a market for large numbers of calculators spurred the manufacturers on to develop even less expensive production techniques. In the space of about two years, the

The race won—man on the moon.

prices of calculators were cut in half. Two years later they were cut in half again, bringing them within the economic reach of just about everyone. Lower and lower the prices dropped until today a simple model can be purchased for under 10 dollars.

The reason for this continual drop in the prices for electronic goods (calculators included) was the further advances in the "state-of-the-art" of solid-state electronic technology. The manufacturers were finding it possible to integrate more and more parts inside a single package. Some of the more recent calculators have been made using one or two large ICs which contain all of the electronic circuits that make the calculator work. This trend eventually led to a manufacturing technique known as "large scale integration" (LSI). It was again inevitable that these new devices

The integrated circuit (IC).

would be incorporated into computers. Since computers consist of many similar circuits they can be fabricated into one small package that functions exactly the same as when separate circuits are used, but is much less costly.

The most significant event that occurred only recently was the advent of the tv or video game. First located in bars, amusement parks, and shopping centers, these most often took the form of a sort of tennis game being played with a small white dot that moved across the screen like a ball. The players operated their paddles by using simple potentiometers or joysticks. In between the potentiometers and the screen were a mass of computer-like electronic circuits that made the whole thing work. Some models even kept score and displayed the numerals on the screen. Again the trend toward denser circuit integration prevailed, and shortly there were tv games on the market that used only one LSI chip. This natu-

The pocket calculator.

rally brought the prices of tv games down to an amount affordable by many people and the home tv game became a popular item.

By the late 1970s, new products were being announced almost every day which were based upon some recent advancement in the state-of-the-art electronics. The once-simple electronic calculator is now capable of performing sophisticated mathematical functions. Some calculators are even programmable by the user to do whatever combination of operations might be needed. We see new wristwatches that no longer have a face and hands but instead

Courtesy National Semiconductor Corp.

Large scale integration.

have glowing red numerals that blink on when the owner's arm is moved. Many modern supermarkets are exchanging their old cash registers for the new electronic versions which do a number of automatic operations while the grocery bill is being tallied. Microwave ovens have built-in memories that can be programmed to turn the oven on at a certain time and cook at a certain temperature for a prescribed length of time. But the most dramatic sign of what this new technology will mean for society is the development and evolution of the personal computer.

A LITTLE HISTORY

The history of the personal computer is one filled with all the thrills of modern capitalism. The history started in 1974 in the deep south of Virginia, where Jonathan Titus, a process control engineer, designed the Mark 8 microcomputer and offered it for sale in the pages of *Radio Electronics* magazine. This was the first

Courtesy Fairchild Camera & Instrument Corp.

The LSI chip.

time a truly low-cost programmable computer was offered for sale to the general public on a national basis. The Mark 8 was in kit form and was very popular among technically oriented people. But the Mark 8 used the new Intel 8008 microprocessor chip, which was rather difficult to program. And since many hobbyists knew that Intel had a more advanced chip, they waited for a product based on the advanced chip.

For most people, 1975 marked the beginning of the microcomputer revolution. In that year a small company called Mits offered

Courtesy Fairchild Camera & Instrument Corp.

The tv game.

a low cost microcomputer kit based on the brand new Intel 8080 chip. An article on how to build the Mits "Altair" 8800 Microcomputer appeared in *Popular Electronics* magazine. The Altair proved to be an instant success, and the company was swamped with hundreds of orders.

The trick to the Altair was that besides using the 8080 chip it possessed a 100-pin edge connector for hooking up multiple boards in the cabinet called the S-100 bus. This meant that hundreds of companies could offer computer boards for Altair owners. This was a great idea and the S-100 bus is still in use today. However, the original S-100 bus was not a well defined standard, some pins were left undefined, others were unclear about timing, etc. Therefore, today the IEEE has produced a more exacting standard called the IEEE-696, but it will be years before all manufacturers adhere to it. Meanwhile it is buyer beware.

Because this market was so untested, the Altair was offered only in kit form. Although it didn't take extraordinary skills to

Digital watch.

Courtesy Novus, Inc.

Courtesy Apple Computer Co.

Portable personal computer.

The first home computer, the Mits Altair 8800B.

build one, it required extreme fortitude to get the complete computer working and to keep it working. Therefore, only sophisticated hobbyists bought Altairs.

The year 1976 marked the first year of explosive growth in the personal computer market. This was the year of Imsai and the i8080, Cromemco, Processor Technology Sol, Polymorphics, Wavemate, The Digital Group, OSI Challenger, M&R Astral 2000, Apple's Apple I, ISC's Intercolor and Compucolor, NorthStar Horizon, and Bally.

Of these companies only OSI, ISC, NorthStar, Apple, and Cromemco survived. At first these computers were only available through mail order ads. Then some actually appeared in the first computer stores, called Byte Shops. You could go in these shops and play with the computer *before* you bought it. However, these computers were still hard to use and only satisfied a certain highly motivated segment of the market, but they served to fire the imagination of a number of computer entrepreneurs. The result was 1977, the first year of the consumer computer.

The year 1977 started off with the first attempt at integrated desktop computers for the home. Apple had a major impact on the market when they brought out the Apple II computer, the first true color computer. The strong sales of the Apple indicated there

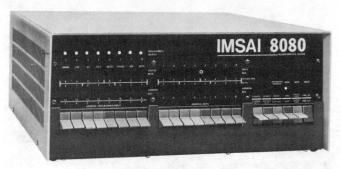

Imsai i8080.

Apple I.

NorthStar Horizon.

Bally arcade.

was a bigger market than had been assumed for this type of home computer.

Then in 1977 the first giant mass market company, Tandy Corporation, entered the personal computer market through its Radio Shack Stores, with a computer under $600 called the TRS-80 Model I. Because the TRS-80 was so low in price and available in over 6000 stores, it was an instant success with consumers, and today Tandy is considered to be the IBM of the home computer industry.

Commodore Business Machines, who had been concentrating on calculators, introduced the PET 2001 which contained its own screen, its own cassette recorder, and a neat tiny calculator-like keyboard. The PET really excited a great number of people, and Commodore's stock jumped so high that Commodore stock trading was halted by the Securities and Exchange Commission. The PET keyboard, being unlike a traditional typewriter, caused controversy. PET was not well supported in the early years, yet it managed to capture the European market. In the same year Heath brought out a computer called the H8, which was in typical par excellence Heathkit format, and Exidy introduced a nice machine called the Sorcerer. The market was heating up. Radio Shack's entry made much larger companies (including IBM) look seriously at the home computer market.

The year that the media discovered the new home computer revolution was also 1977. Articles touted the new changes that the computers would bring to people's lives. Computer books by the dozen appeared. New computer book publishers were born overnight: Osbourn, Schelbi, Sybex, Dilithium, and Creative Computing Press (all still here). Magazines by the dozen appeared: *Byte*, *Creative Computing*, *Kilobaud*, *Personal Computing*, and *Intelligent Machines Journal* (now *Info World*). All kinds of self teaching books on computers, like *Your Own Computer*, made it easy for many people to learn what amazing things you could do with a computer today.

A small company called Digital Research began distributing a special kind of universal program (called an operating system) for use on the growing number of S-100 computers. Recall, all kinds of companies were making boards for S-100 computer owners so the buyer had a great range of products to choose from. This operating system was called CP/M (Control Program for Microcomputers).

Apple II.

Radio ShackTRS-80 Model I.

Commodore PET 2001.

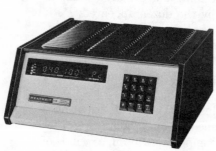

Heath H8.

Exidy Sorcerer.

22

Soon, many people were writing programs that could run on CP/M equipped computers, and this spawned more sales of CP/M based computers, until CP/M went on to become the defacto standard operating system in the micro community. Today, CP/M is threatened by a better operating system called UNIX, that was invented at Bell Telephone Labs. CP/M is fighting back with a version for the 8086 16-bit chip called CP/M-86, along with CP/Net and MP/M.

Companies such as Dynabyte, Vector Graphics, and Altos appeared with computers that ran CP/M. Several new software companies thrived on the new body of S-100 computer owners, including Structured Systems, which began offering professional programs for CP/M based microcomputers and Microsoft, which began producing high level language BASIC interpreters for microcomputers. Soon, almost all personal computers hosted Microsoft BASIC in one of three versions. Not all manufacturers revealed this, however.

Helping the sale of business systems that used CP/M, and computers like the Apple, was a new type of retail computer store called Computerland. These appeared across the country to help people buy and learn about low cost home computers. Today, there is a Computerland in almost every major city, and many more are planned. Other types of computer stores are starting up, including a unique franchised approach called On-Line stores.

By 1979 a number of large companies entered the market and some early companies, like Imsai and Mits died. Atari, an expert in the television and arcade video game market, brought out their first home computer, a powerful color unit with strong graphic ability, called the Atari 400 and 800. The desktop color computer was becoming the major configuration. The product from Texas Instruments, the TI 99/4, fell into this category. The TI 99/4 color desktop computer even offered a speech output capability. Similarly, AFP, the giant home entertainment corporation, introduced the Imagination Machine. Everybody was talking about the computer market, including Wall Street. Tandy had become a hot stock. Radio Shack had introduced a Model II unit with extended BASIC and a Level III small business system. By the end of 1979 the personal computer was moving out of the fun and games market into a more professional market. People were seeking more productive uses for the computer, such as accounting and word

Atari 400.

Texas Instruments 99/4.

APF Imagination Machine.

Radio Shack TRS-80 Model II.

processing. The hardware was getting so advanced that the manufacturers could not produce enough software products to take advantage of this power and satisfy the growing number of users. It took a very great effort to produce a really good and practical software program and only a small number of the major manufacturers were attempting to deal with this crisis. It was the hobbyist in the microcomputer community who actually produced the first real unique software products.

It became apparent that a good "generic" software program was needed that could solve a wide range of problems, but could be reconfigured by different users to provide for different applications that would easily run on different computers. Thus, Visicalc, Desk Top Plan, WordStar, Electric Pencil, and other very well designed programs were created. These systems had a stimulating effect on the market, showing what a computer was truly capable of.

With the coming of a new decade, the major manufacturers, like Atari, Tandy, Apple, and Commodore, were looking hard at products more geared to the business and professional markets. It seemed that now more practical uses of the computer, ones that actually saved money or time, could make or break the sale of the hardware. In the 1980s we saw the beginning of substantial program offerings from the various manufacturers. We also saw the major publishers jump into the microcomputer market. McGraw-Hill purchased Microcomputer publisher Adam Osbourn and the popular *Byte* magazine for untold millions, and Howard W. Sams presented its line of circuit design software programs. We also saw the fist re-birth of a microcomputer company as a dynamic man and wife team called Fischer/Frietas started up Imsai again.

WHERE ARE WE NOW?

Today, the personal computer market is a billion dollar per year market, and is still undergoing major growing pains. In 1980 four large companies entered the market, including Mattel with the Intellivision, multibillion dollar Hewlett-Packard with the HP-85 (very expensive and very professional), Zenith Systems with an assembled Z-89 (which was an assembled Heath H-89—Zenith bought out Heath), and Sinclair Limited with the ZX-80 book-size computer.

Apple introduced the Apple III in late 1980, touting it as a professional computer for word processing or business accounting with identical features as the Apple II (meaning it could use all that computer's software), but with more power and capability. Sinclair surprised everyone with a book size, mail order computer for under $200 that spoke BASIC, and worked with a television. But it was Tandy that overwhelmed the industry with the introduction of *three* new computer models in late 1980. There was a TRS-80 Color Computer, a TRS-80 Pocket Computer, and a TRS-80 Model III, which was a much better engineered Model I. Tandy, basically, offered a computer in all the possible configurations of the day.

What are the hardware configurations of the various personal and small business computers on the market today? Usually, you can fit the product into one of three different categories. The first category is the (new) pocket, or handheld, computer. These computers, like the Tandy Pocket Computer, are small enough to fit into a purse, use a flat LCD display, and can run small BASIC programs. They represent the shape of the future.

The next category for a configuration is the desktop computer. The desktop is usually small and naturally fits on a desktop. It is often a color unit, like the Apple, the Atari, and the TI; but it may also be in one color or black and white like the PET, HP, and TRS-80 Models I and II. The desktop computer may, or may not, have all components integrated into one package.

The third category is the mainframe computers. Manufacturers do not like this name, but it more clearly signifies that these are larger computers with frames for holding the various circuit boards that make up the computer system. Here, companies like North-Star and Cromemco are flourishing because there are hundreds of companies selling S-100 hardware boards and CP/M software.

There is also a major personal computer peripherals market developing, as more and more manufacturers bring out products that run on other companies' computers. This symbiotic relationship means cheaper products are available for the consumer.

Of course, not all computers fall nicely into these categories— handheld, desktop, mainframe—but they do cover a vast majority of the configurations that you will find today. In Chapter 5 we will examine the insides of these computers. But as we will see, in the future the actual hardware that comprises the computer may be vastly different.

Zenith data systems
Z—89.

Hewlett-Packard HP-85.

Apple III.

Mattel Intellivision.

Sinclair ZX-80.

Radio Shack TRS-80 Pocket computer.

**Radio Shack TRS-80 color
computer.**

Radio Shack Model III.

27

WHAT'S COMING IN 1990?

Making a predication for the future of the home, or personal, computer is a dangerous and bold undertaking. It is equivalent to trying to say where the human race will be in the future. Beyond 10 years it is most difficult to say. However, given that most scientists suffer both failure of nerve and failure of imagination when it comes to projecting the future, we will let our imagination flow more freely. We will start by understanding that the computer is headed towards being a product of extreme importance in helping its owner live and interact in the world. Before you scream shades of a computerized and helpless society, examine the kinds of things that members of a junior college English class in a large city said they would like a computer to do for them if they were to buy one.

The women in the class were most interested. They wanted the computer to be pocket size, nice looking with pretty colors, and fit in a purse. The things they wanted it to do include having it tell them the best restaurants for certain kinds of foods and entertainment reports about shows, dances, music, etc. Instructions on how to get to these places of business were mentioned as important. The women in the class wanted the computer to allow them to match up with men with similar interests, perhaps via the telephone, and to be able to read about the other person (or hopefully persons) in the morning, in privacy. Where to buy clothes and groceries was important, as were the stores with the best buys, the latest styles, and the prices so the same computer could examine their budgets and come up with advice on how to buy the right items. They wanted the computer to be benevolent, friendly, fatherly, and infallible; in short, close to perfect. The computer could be authoritative *if* they felt it was deserved. The computer would have a personality something akin to R2-D2, only a little more mature.

The men, and some of the women, were interested in the style also, but they preferred a more masculine appearance. However, the functions they wanted included the entertainment features that the women pointed out. Both groups wished that the computer could help them in getting through school. It was assumed by the students throughout the discussion that the means of giving information to the computer could be by a typewriter keyboard or by the computer recognizing speech. All preferred speech. As students they thought it would be nice for them to be able to do homework on the computer, and turn it into the teacher on a tiny tape cassette or something similar. In terms of the computer communicating with the students, most preferred spoken communications mixed with a graphics display of pictures. However, regular text output on a flat screen, mixed with some graphics, was also acceptable for many.

What does this tell us about where the computer is going? It shows us that the computer will eventually have to be able to serve as an extremely functional, practical, and useful machine that will be used by everyone on a daily basis, if it is to capture the interest of the future adults of this country. For a computer to do most of these desirable functions, it would not be unreasonable for the product to cost *more than one thousand dollars*. Since people spend such amounts on automobiles, it is likely they would spend the same on a device that brought nearly the same kinds of rewards that a car does. The automobile brings power of mobility to the owner. When the computer reaches the point that it offers the same power, it will truly be a mass market item.

As far as its physical attributes, the trend is for the personal computer to become much smaller in the near future. A trend has already begun, as witnessed by the Tandy Pocket Computer, and the Sinclair book size unit (see Chapter 6 for a detailed examination of these products). The real miniaturization, however, will probably come from Japan. Execution of a product design, rather than the innovation of new ideas, has always been the pride of the Japanese, and so it is very probable that we will see Japan take over the personal computer market, just as they took over transistor radios, economy cars, calculators, and steel production. American manufacturers will most likely remain the leader in innovative design of personal computer products. But the Japanese manufacturers will probably become the leaders in sales of these products. Of course, this doesn't mean that America will lose the computer market. The consumer will profit greatly from the competition.

It is likely that the personal computer will soon have a flat panel liquid crystal display (LCD) like the kind now used in digital watches, but larger and more complex. The display will most likely be in color. A recent display technology convention in Japan revealed that the flat panel screen for Japanese automobiles is right around the corner. Computers will follow. The screen will most likely allow high resolution graphics and pictures to be displayed. Someday, if the crystals can be made to change from light to dark fast enough, we might see the computer serve also as a television or video cassette player. This would allow us to transmit pictures along with data—important for the entertainment and dating functions that were discussed previously.

Further, we can expect that the future personal computer will have an advanced form of mass storage, such as a miniature hard disk with backup ability on a lower cost device. Today, 5¼-inch Winchester hard disks are appearing with over 5 megabytes of storage. Perhaps streaming cassette tape, which today can store 10 megabytes in 5 minutes, will be the way things will go. The streaming cassette tape will be small, cheap, and will serve as a transport medium for programs and functions. You could mail them easily.

There is a good chance that future home and personal computers will have built-in modems. A modem allows the computer to communicate with other computers over the telephone. The huge array of installed telephones, each with a computer attached to it, makes up a fantastic communication "network" with powerful attributes. You could, for example, leave your computer to search through the night for anyone within a 100 mile radius offering an early 1970 red Volkswagen for sale that cost under $1000. The computer would inform the network of its need, and search for the desired seller, all automatically. In the morning a list of near hits and actual finds would be generated.

There is a strong possibility that the am-fm stereo radio may eventually be built into the personal computer. After all, the technology for reproducing music is very similar to the technology for recording computer data and to the technology for generating speech—most computers of the future will speak to you. Plastic records may die out and be replaced by tiny information disks that are streaming tape cartridges that contain hundreds of songs. The Screen Actors Guild may be back on strike as the rights and royalties to this type of storage medium are worked out. Since copying software is a computer's forte, it may be that the complexities of protecting programs slows down their advancement, but probably not by much.

We can also expect to see the personal computer performing language translation for its user. This will mean that other countries will not seem so foreign, as their languages become understandable to all. Perhaps this is the key to the global society—a sort of universal world language spoken through computers.

Of course, all this will take years to accomplish, but the hint of such capability are already appearing. We have speech output capabilities, and talking televisions and calculators have been demonstrated. It is the cost of memory devices that prohibits widespread use of speech output today. But since the cost of computer memory chips is falling at a very fast clip, it won't be long before this, too, is no longer a limiting factor.

Many of the features we have described are based on the ability to fill the computer with information from the outside world on a regular basis (recall being able to find the restaurant or clothing store sale on the pocket computer). Success will require that stores make such data available to thousands of computers. Today, we use the newspaper to find this information and one must scan it visually to find what is wanted. This is a slow and inefficient process—just the job for computers.

A solution may be to have the newspaper information put over the telephone line or airwaves so everyone's computer could receive the same enormous bulk of data *but only store that which the computer owner wants.* Or perhaps services will appear that mail cassette cartridges out to subscribers who then place the cartridges in their computers and have them scan the data for them. Imagine a world where instead of having to wait 24 hours for news by newspaper, or waiting for the news on television, you will have instant access to events as they occur! The response time of the computer receiver may be 360 times faster than the normal newspaper.

Our point is that in the future the computer will occupy an enormously complex and involved role in the daily life of human beings. Trying to imagine what the future will be like is very difficult, but it is absolutely safe to say that the world will never be the same!

CHAPTER 2

Computer Vocabulary

Like most specialized fields, the computer world has its own jargon. If you are with some people who are into computers, chances are much of what they talk about is a mystery to you. This small glossary and table of acronyms has been compiled near the beginning of this book so that you can get some fast insights before proceeding on your journey. If you are already familiar with the meaning of such words as "bootstrap" and "firmware" then you will probably go on to the next chapter.

A

A/D Conversion—An A/D (Analog/Digital) conversion measures an input voltage level, and then outputs a digitally encoded number corresponding to the voltage. This provides a relatively simple way to get signals from the outside world to the inside of a computer. "That's the fastest *A/D conversion* I've ever seen."

Algorithm—The sequence of steps to be followed to arrive at a solution to a problem. It is usually a programming procedure that uses "iteration" to produce the desired result. Frequently algorithms are named after their originators. "The *Widro-Hoff LMS algorithm* is a programming procedure that removes 'noise' from a signal."

Alphanumeric —The set of symbols containing the letters A-Z (alpha) and the numbers 0-9 (numeric), as well as special punctuation characters. "Most computers use *alphanumeric* characters."

Applications Program—A program that actually solves a specific problem, as opposed to the programs that perform system functions, such as assemblers, etc. "The *applications program* is rather long."

Assembler—A system program that allows programming in the mnemonic codes of assembly language. Assembler programs are one step above binary machine-language programming. "Many computer hobbyists use *assemblers*."

Assembly Language—A low-level symbolic programming language, that uses mnemonic codes such as ADD, LDA, SUB, etc. Historically the first programming aid. "What is the *assembly language* format for add?"

ASCII Character—Short for *A*merican *S*tandard *C*ode for *I*nformation *I*nterchange, ASCII is the most widely recognized 8-bit code for representing alphanumerics of the English language. Pronounced "*ask-ee.*" "The *ASCII* code for 7 is 00110111."

B

BASIC—Stands for *B*eginners *A*ll purpose *S*ymbolic *I*nstruction *C*ode. BASIC is a widely used beginners high-level programming language. Like most high-level languages, it uses powerful statements like "10 PRINT X/Y + 1" rather than machine codes or mnemonics. "Hobbyists love *BASIC* because it's so much like English."

Baud Rate—The number of bits per second a computer is capable of sending or receiving. Baud rate usually varies from 300 (teletypewriter speed) to 9600. "The *baud rate* of a typical computer is 300."

Binary—The base-two number system which uses the digits 0 and 1. The first four numbers in binary are 00, 01, 10, 11. Computers use binary because electronic components can be made cheaply to switch between two states such as +5 volts and ground. "To get a feeling for how computers calculate, try counting in *binary*."

Bit—A contraction of the words *B*inary dig*IT*, a bit is the smallest unit of computer information. Several bits together make up a letter, number, or word. "Eight *bits* is a byte."

Bootstrap—The general technique of using one thing to aid in the start of another thing. In computers, a short program that allows a larger program to be entered into the computer. "First load the *bootstrap* loader, then load the program."

Branch—The process of taking a departure from the normal sequence of operations in a computer program. Also a programmed jump based on continuous testing in the computer program. "Computers make good use of *branch* instructions, such as BNE (branch on not equal)."

Bug—Something which causes the computer program to malfunction. Usually, but not always, due to an error in the logic of the program. "Not another *bug!*"

Byte—A group of adjacent bits. A specific portion of a binary word. The most common size byte is 8 bits, although 16 is also used, as well as 4 and 12. "I always think of a *byte* as 8 bits."

Buffer—A temporary storage location for holding a number of bits. For instance a keyboard buffer may hold several ASCII characters, each of which is 8 bits long. "Your *buffer* overflowed."

C

Chip — Another word for "integrated circuit," this is a technique where thousands of electronic semiconductor components can be mass produced on a tiny piece of silicon (sand). "Did you know there's a *chip* in your telephone, and one in your car, and one in your watch?"

COBOL — Generally found in operation on large computer systems, COBOL is a high-level programming language that is geared more toward business applications. "There is a great need for *COBOL* programmers in business."

Collate — To compare or merge two things into one thing. Usually refers to files in the computer. "Lets *collate* the data."

Compiler — A compiler is a computer program. Its purpose is to convert high-level language statements typed in at a keyboard to machine code for the computer. "*Compilers* are more efficient than 'Interpreters' when it comes to saving memory space."

Complement — The number produced by performing a basic operation on the original number. In binary the complement of a number is found by reversing all the digits, i.e., 101 complemented is 010. "Certain computer instruction codes *complement* a number in a register."

Core Memory — The early computers used little doughnuts of ferrite material to store bits. Because ferrite is a magnetic material a core memory doesn't forget its contents. Bubble memory may revive the concept of core memory. "Time to do a *core* dump, and find out what's in it."

Console — The part of a computer system that is used for communication between the operator and the system. The console usually contains switches, lights, and keyboards specifically for man-machine communication. "As usual the *console* is dead."

CP/M — A widely used group of programs that facilitates the utilization of floppy disk as a mass storage device. It allows for files to be created, manipulated, and erased from the disk, or to be transferred from one disk to another. "Much of the application software that is on the market today is designed to use *CP/M*."

CRT Display — A type of computer terminal that displays information on a television-like screen. This screen is the face of a cathode ray tube (CRT). "That's really a fast *CRT*, but I don't like the green characters."

D

Debug — The art of removing errors, or "bugs," from a computer program. Usually the crucial stage in developing a good program. Unfortunately, not all bugs are always found. "Always allow at least 10 minutes per BASIC statement, for *debugging*."

Disk —A type of mass storage technique that stores information on magnetically sensitive surfaces, about the size of a 45-rpm record. "The cheapest form of mass storage in 1977 was the floppy *disk*."

Dos —Stands for *D*isk *O*perating *S*ystem. A computer system that uses a magnetic disk to contain all the routines and programs that run the computer. An FDOS is a floppy disk-based DOS. "Soon there will be Bubble Operating Systems, and the *DOS* will be obsolete."

Dump —The action of causing the pattern of binary bits in a computer to be displayed on an output device. "By doing a *dump* we'll determine the bad bit."

Dynamic Memory —A type of memory arrangement where all the various memory cells must be refreshed every so often so they keep their proper state. Although a less-power-consuming form of memory than static memory, dynamic memory requires complex addressing circuits. "Sometimes you hear about pseudo-*dynamic* memory."

E

Editor —A special computer program that allows changing, moving, and general editing of statements. Editing is a simple form of word processing, but is often reserved for changing assembly statements. "An *editor* is a fantastic tool for fixing computer programs."

Eighty-eighty (8080) —This was one of the first microprocessors that really took the world by storm. The single LSI chip contains a complete MPU. "The *8080* is used in many computers."

EPROM —Stands for *E*lectrically *P*rogrammable *R*ead *O*nly *M*emory. A type of memory that can hold data forever. EPROMs are programmed by an electrical process that establishes each bit as a 1 or a 0. EPROMs are often used to hold the monitor or operating system programs. "You can buy special EPROM programmers, but they are expensive."

F

File —A sequence of related records, frequently found in floppy disk, cassette, or mass storage systems. A file is an abstract name for an aggregation of data sets in the form of a series of characters or bits which together may describe some quantity or numeric value. "The disk has fantastic *file* commands."

Firmware —Software or programs that are permanently stored in ROM or EPROM. Also any microprogram that causes a machine to emulate a certain instruction set. "The nice thing about firmware is that you can easily change it (compared to changing hardware)."

Floppy Disk —Disk storage where the magnetic medium is located on small flexible disks, which are encased in a protective cardboard container. Floppies are somewhat slower than "hard" disks, they wear faster, but are less costly. "Wait till they make a micro-*floppy* disk."

Flowchart—A diagram that represents the logic and reasoning behind a program or a circuit. "Programmers are always forgetting to *flowchart* their programs."

FORTRAN—Stands for *FOR*mula *TRAN*slation, and refers to a computer language that is used for computational-type programming, especially when involving algebraic problems. A compiler language. "*FORTRAN* is almost as easy as BASIC, but much more mathematical."

H

Handshaking Logic—A type of computer interface design where the computer sends a signal, and waits until the interface sends a signal back signifying it is done. The back and forth communication is like shaking hands. "*Handshaking Logic* makes troubleshooting easy."

Hard Disk—For years the standard on the big systems, the hard disk is starting to find its way into the microcomputer field. As the name implies, the disk is similar to a "floppy" disk, except it isn't floppy, it is "hard." "A *hard disk* system will be more reliable than floppy disk."

Hex—Short for hexadecimal, the base-16 number-system is commonly used in computers because it is easier to remember FF than 11111111. "Compared to binary, *hex* is much easier to work with."

Heuristic—A special program that has the ability to alter itself to improve itself. Often associated with artificial intelligence (AI), heuristics are used in many non-AI computer programs. "I really enjoy chess playing *heuristics*."

I

IC—Stands for *I*ntegrated *C*ircuit. *See* Chip.

Instruction Set—The "menu" of instructions a computer can execute. Unless computers have identical instruction sets, they cannot run the same programs. "The XYZ-80 has over 180 instructions."

Interface—A circuit that allows one type of electronic unit to communicate with another electronic or mechanical device. Chiefly used as a buffer between computers and mechanical devices. "Better check the serial *interface*."

Interpreter—A computer program that converts high-level-language statements to "machine" code for direct computer operation. Unlike a compiler, however, it executes the statements immediately, instead of later. BASIC is an interpreter language. "Most *interpreter* languages are slow."

Interrupt—An external event that overrides any current computer action and causes a certain special program to be run. Frequently "priorities" are established among interrupts so that several devices can interrupt a computer. "Do computers mind being *interrupted?*"

I/O —Stands for *I*nput/*O*utput. A generalized expression for the action of sending information into a computer (I or Input) and getting it out of the computer (O or Output). "Try wiggling the *I/O* cable."

L

LCD —*L*iquid *C*rystal *D*isplay is an everyday encounter with all of the new digital watches using it instead of LED (light emitting diode) displays. "Soon we will have *LCD* panels as display devices instead of tv."

Looping —A programming technique where a portion of a program is repeated over and over, until a certain result is obtained. "Try *looping* until the bit goes high."

LSI —Stands for *L*arge *S*cale *I*ntegration. A way of making denser and more complex integrated circuits. Eventually LSI will be replaced by VLSI (*V*ery *L*arge *S*cale *I*ntegration), and VLSI by ELSI (*E*xtremely *L*arge *S*cale *I*ntegration). "General Motors uses advanced *LSI*-hybrid circuits in fuel regulators."

Line Printer —A very high speed printer output device that can type text at several hundred lines per minute. A very expensive computer peripheral, but also a very powerful one. "I would buy a *line printer* if I could sell some service and make a profit to pay it off."

M

Machine Language —The lowest level of computer programming; this is the only language the computer can understand without the aid of another program. Looks like: . . . FF FF FF FF B8 C9 D9 C0 . . . "Programming in *machine language* isn't quite so bad."

Macro —Short for macroinstruction. An instruction that generates a larger sequence of instructions. "Good assemblers have many *macros.*"

Microprocessor —All the essential electronics of a computer miniaturized to a single chip the size of a pin head. Contained usually in an IC package with 18 to 40 leads. "*Microprocessors* keep getting smaller."

Mini-Floppy —A small floppy disk. About 5 inches in diameter, these mini-floppy disks can't store as much information as the standard 8-inch type. They are less expensive, however. "The system I am getting has dual *mini-floppies.*"

Mnemonic —Pronounced "new-monic." A short word or group of letters that stands for another word, and is easy to remember. For instance, "Add X to the Accumulator" might be abbreviated "ADDX." "This computer has elegant *mnemonics.*"

Modem —Stands for *MO*dulator *DEM*odulator. Usually connects between the computer and telephone line and converts digital signals to audio tones and vice versa. "A good *modem* is simple to use."

MPU —Stands for *M*icro *P*rocessor *U*nit. Another way to say microprocessor. "Motorola makes an *MPU* called the 6800."

N

Nanosecond—One billionth of a second, or 1/1000 of a microsecond. "Some of today's faster personal computers operate in the *nanosecond* range."

Nested Program—A program which is contained as a part of another larger program. "The printing subroutine is *nested* within the main program."

Network—An interconnected group of computers, terminals, or even telephones. "Computer *networks* are becoming more and more popular."

NOP Instruction—A computer instruction which has no effect on computer operation, and is therefore called a no-op. These are often used to reserve space within a program for possible future expansion. "Leave a *NOP instruction* after the last byte of the program."

Nonvolatile Memory—A form of computer memory that will store information for an indefinite period of time with no power applied. "Magnetic core is *nonvolatile memory*, as are ROMs and EPROMS."

O

Object Program—A program that is in machine executable form. This means that the program is most likely to be in some sort of a binary pattern, ready to be used by the computer. "Object programs are very difficult for the average person to understand."

Octal—A number system based upon the number 8. There are eight digits in the octal system—0 through 7. "The use of the *octal* system makes programming easier than when using binary."

Off-Line—Refers to computer equipment which is not at the time directly connected to the computer. "Take the printer *off-line* for a minute."

On-Line—Describes the condition of a piece of computer equipment which is directly connected to the computer. "This system has 5 megabytes of *on-line* disk storage."

Operand—The object or "target" of some program operation, usually a number or variable that is involved in some arithmetic operation. "The *operand* of that instruction has not been defined."

Operating System—A group of special programs that are used in various combinations to make a computer easier to use. "Some computers have very flexible *operating systems*."

Operation Code—Sometimes referred to as "Op-code" this is the electronic binary pattern that directs the computer circuits to perform some particular operation. "The *Op-code* for an ADD instruction is 11000101."

Overflow—The result of performing an arithmetic operation within the computer which yields an answer that is too large to be contained in the MPU. "Adding two large numbers together may cause an *overflow* to occur."

P

Page —A term often used in conjunction with computer memory. A memory page contains some fixed number of bytes. "The keyboard input buffer occupies one *page* of memory."

Paper-Tape —A means of storing binary information by punching small holes in a continuous strip of paper. This is most common in teletypewriter-related equipment. "Many programs are available on *paper-tape*."

Parallel —Pertaining to events that occur simultaneously. Most commonly used in conjunction with the transmission of binary information, where all the bits of a given byte are sent at the same time. "The ASCII keyboard is a *parallel* device."

Parameter —A special element of data that is to be used as a condition for some type of processing. "There are several *parameters* involved in processing this data."

Parity —A means of determining the validity of computer data stored in binary. "A *parity* error occurred while reading the data."

Pascal —A powerful new high-level language that combines all of the best features and capabilities of BASIC, FORTRAN, and COBOL. It is becoming available on many small computers. "Perhaps *Pascal* would be a good language to program it in."

Patch —A quick change to an existing program to cause it to operate differently. "Let's *patch* in a jump instruction at a key point."

Peripheral —A device which is connected to the computer in order to provide communication with the real world. "There are many different kinds of *peripherals* available for your personal computer."

Photoelectric —Pertaining to the use of light to detect the presence or absence of holes in paper tape, or punched cards. "*Photoelectric* readers are faster than mechanical ones."

Picosecond —One-millionth of a microsecond, or 1/1000th of a nanosecond. "A *picosecond* is almost too small an interval of time to conceive."

PL-1 —A very powerful high-level programming language, generally found in use on large computer systems, but which will inevitably be used with the personal computer. "Programming in *PL-1* is a snap."

Program —A set of instructions that defines a particular process that the computer is to perform. The program can take many different forms from the original written specifications to the actual binary instructions that the MPU will execute. "The first step will be to load the *program* into the computer."

R

Random Access —Pertains to the storage of data in memory of some sort. Random access means being able to access any location of memory individually, as opposed to "serial access" memory which requires that the memory locations be accessed in sequence. "Floppy disks are *random access* devices."

Read—To sense, or obtain the state of the data either in memory, or from an input device. "*Read* in the program from cassette tape."

Real-Time—An expression used in discussing a type of computer operation in which the computer is interacting with events in the world of people, rather than of circuits. Generally speaking, the interaction must take place in a fast enough time so as to be able to influence or react to the particular "people" event in progress. "The computer can monitor the apparatus in *real-time*."

Record—An assemblage of several data elements that are all in some way related, and are handled as a unit. "How many *records* can the disk file contain?"

Register—An electronic circuit within the microprocessing unit that is capable of storing one or more bytes of information. The most common register is the accumulator register, in which all of the arithmetic operations are performed. "When the operation is complete, the result will be in the A register."

Routine—A group of program instructions which accomplishes a particular task that needs to be done frequently. A group of instructions can be used over and over again, simply by referring to it from another part of the program. "Write a *routine* that finds the largest of five numbers."

S

Seek-Time—The length of time required to find a record of data, generally with reference to disk files. "The average *seek-time* for a good floppy disk is in the millisecond range."

Sequence—Pertaining to the order that things (bits, bytes, records, or files) are arranged. "It may be important to maintain alphabetic *sequence* in some applications."

Serial—An arrangement where one element of data is linked to the next so that progress must start at the beginning and proceed from the first element through the next, and on to the finish, never skipping any. "Cassette tape files are stored in *serial* form on the tape."

Sixteen-Bit Microprocessor—Many of the newer computers are using the new microprocessor units that operate within a 16-bit instruction set. These can also address more memory than the 8-bit MPUs and will make a computer much faster. "Maybe we should look for a computer with a *16-bit microprocessor*."

Sixty-Five-Oh-Two (6502)—This is a microprocessor chip that was developed along the lines of the Motorola 6800. It also used the "tri-state logic" method of interfacing to the buses. "Many personal computers utilize the *6502* chip."

Software—A nickname given to computer programs, which, of course, are not composed of electronic circuits, or hardware. "There is a lot of *software* available for some personal computers."

Statement—Often used when discussing high-level languages such as BASIC. A BASIC statement is a single unit of program command, of which there are many making up the entire program. "The PRINT *statement* causes the data to be displayed on the video display."

Storage—Sometimes used as a synonym for memory. This might be "core storage" or "disk storage" or any other form of computer memory. "There is a lot of space for program *storage* on a floppy disk."

Store—The act of saving some data in a computer memory. The data can then later be "retrieved" or "read" and used in further operations. "*Store* the results of the test in memory."

Streaming Tape—A new technique of recording binary data on magnetic tape at very high speeds. This is especially useful when using magnetic tape as a backup medium for disk files. "The ideal system would be a 5 megabyte hard disk with a *streaming tape*."

Subroutine—*See* Routine.

System—A group of programs and subroutines that are all related to processing for a particular application area. "There are good general ledger *systems* available for CPAs."

T

Terminal—An Input/Output device that can be connected to a computer in order to communicate with it and control processing. "A common *terminal* consists of an ASCII keyboard and a video display."

Time-Sharing—A process in which a single computer divides its time among several tasks to be done. This makes it appear as if all the tasks were being processed simultaneously. "The cost of *time-sharing* on a large computer decreases as the number of people sharing the time increases."

U

Update—To make current. As with programs that have been modified to comply with some change in circumstances. Or, any form of data, such as a disk file record, might be renewed with more current information. "It is important to *update* your system as new features become available."

V

Video Display—A computer output device which presents the data to the user in the form of a television picture. This picture can either be in the form of printed characters, or as a video image of some sort. "One drawback of *video displays* is that there is no hard copy."

Volatile—Pertaining to the characteristic of certain types of computer memory which lose their contents when power is removed. "All of the application programs can be stored in *volatile* memory."

W

Winchester Drive — A hard disk drive mechanism that is completely sealed with the disk inside. This prevents contamination from the environment and damage due to excessive handling. "If the system had *Winchester drives*, it wouldn't have so many data errors."

Word — A term used for years in the computer world to describe a logical group of bits. "The term 'byte' has become dominant for the term *word* in personal computing."

Write — Often used synonymously with "store," this word means to deposit data into some form of computer memory. This might be magnetic memory, or disk memory, or writing information onto magnetic tape. "Data can be read back after we *write* it onto the disk."

Z

Z-80 — This is a beefed up version of the 8080 microprocessor chip. It has faster speed, and a larger number of instructions than it can perform. "The new intelligent terminals are *Z-80* based."

PERSONAL COMPUTING ACRONYMS

AC — Alternating Current
ACC — Accumulator
A/D — Analog to Digital
BCD — Binary Coded Decimal
BPS — Bits Per Second
CCD — Charge Coupled Device
CMOS — Complementary MOS
CPS — Characters Per Second
CPU — Central Processing Unit
CR — Carriage Return
CRT — Cathode Ray Tube
D/A — Digital to Analog
DC — Direct Current
DIP — Dual In Line Package
DMA — Direct Memory Access
ECL — Emitter Coupled Logic
EPROM — Electrically Programmable ROM
EOR — Exclusive OR
FAMOS — Floating Gate Avalanche-Injection MOS
FET — Field Effect Transistor
FIFO — First In First Out
GIGO — Old Programmers Adage: "Garbage In, Garbage Out"
GP — General Purpose
HEX — Hexadecimal

I/O — Input/Output
IC — Integrated Circuit (Chip)
INT — Interrupt
I^2L — Integration Injection Logic
K — 1024
LED — Light Emitting Diode
LIFO — Last In First Out
LP — Line Printer
LPM — Lines Per Minute
LSB — Least Significant Bit
LSI — Large Scale Integration
MPU — Microprocessor Unit
MOS — Metal Oxide Semiconductor
MSB — Most Significant Bit
MSI — Medium Scale Integration
MUX — Multiplexer
NMOS — N-Channel MOS
OV — Overflow
PC — Personal Computer
PC — Program Counter
PLA — Programmable Logic Array
PMOS — P-Channel MOS
POS — Point-Of-Scale
PROM — Programmable ROM
PSW — Program Status Word
Q — Positive Logic Output of a Flip-Flop

$\bar{Q}$ —Negative Logic Output of a Flip-Flop (also called "not Q")

RAM —Random Access Memory

ROM —Read Only Memory

RTC —Real Time Clock

R/W —Read/Write

SOS —Silicon On Sapphire

SR —Shift Register

SSI —Small Scale Integration

SUB —Subroutine

TSS —Time-Sharing System

TTY —Teletypewriter

TTL —Transistor Transistor Logic

UART —Universal Asynchronous Receiver Transmitter

USART —Universal Synchronous-Asynchronous Receiver Transmitter

X —Index

XOR —Exclusive OR

CHAPTER 3

Personal Computer Applications

IN YOUR HOME

The home is where your personal computer will most likely be born. If you decide to build it yourself, it will undoubtedly be "fired up" in your workshop and tested for a while before you begin to put it to work. If you buy it preassembled you will want to begin using the various programs that come with it. Once you have determined that everything seems to be working correctly, you can plan on setting up some kind of simple function to start. As you develop more skills with your personal computer, you can move on to bigger and better things.

The Home Accountant

There are many ways in which you can use a personal computer to aid you in financial matters. Accounting is a discipline which requires a precise approach to mathematics (something by which the computer comes naturally)—for example, the monthly routine of balancing your checkbook. This is something which could not only be more accurate with a computer, but would also be more fun! To begin with, you would have to establish your current balance by hand, and enter it into the computer. Then, each month (or other convenient interval) you would have to enter into your computer the following information:

1. The amounts of any deposits.
2. The amounts of all the checks you have written.
3. The amounts of any "bank entries."
4. The numbers of the canceled checks which you have received from the bank.

Then, faster than you can blink an eye, your personal computer will tell you your current balance.

This procedure could be done every day if desired, thereby giving you up-to-the-minute information regarding the state of your checking account. This kind of information is essential for good budget planning and expense control. You can easily determine your spending habits and even see how to save money.

Income Tax Filing

Income taxes are another area where your personal computer can save you a great deal of time, and maybe even some money. Whether you itemize your deductions or file the short form, your home computer can be like having your own personal accountant. The big problem with income tax preparation is that most people put it off until the last minute, and then have to wade through mountains of receipts and canceled checks to derive the various deductions. This procedure is something that your personal computer can do automatically during the entire year so that when the time comes, all you have to do is simply instruct the computer to produce an itemized listing of deductions. Once your taxable income has been computed, your personal computer can use its internal tax tables to figure your tax. It can even fill out your tax return forms for you so that all you have to do is sign them and drop them in the mail. In addition, your personal computer can save this information for as long as you want. Your home computer can also be used to estimate your income tax liability for the next year, so that there will not be any surprises regarding your taxes. In addition, saving all this information in your personal computer can provide for automatic calculation of depreciation of capital assets, as well as amortization schedules for any kind of loan payments and interest rates.

Management of Domestic Resources

Resource management is an area where the personal computer really shines. In an age when we see our world rapidly shrinking,

The home accountant.

and our necessary resources diminishing, we need to become more efficient in our use of such things as energy, water, food, and time. Your personal computer can be of great assistance in these areas. One thing that it can do with ease is to keep track of the food that you have on hand, and help you to plan meals more efficiently in order to eliminate waste. As certain items in the kitchen become depleted, the computer can provide you with a shopping list. About the only thing that your personal computer cannot do is wash the dishes . . . yet.

Besides being able to do all of the foregoing, your personal computer can also continuously monitor the use of other valuable resources around the home. It can be connected to the electrical system and automatically turn on or off any circuit you desire. It can even be used to randomly turn lights on and off in your home while you are away. In fact, your personal computer makes an ideal central control point for a home intruder alarm system. And this is only the beginning. Once you have your own computer, you will be thinking of all kinds of ways that it can be useful to you.

FOR FUN

The fun aspect of having a personal computer is probably the greatest reason they have become so popular. They are fun to read

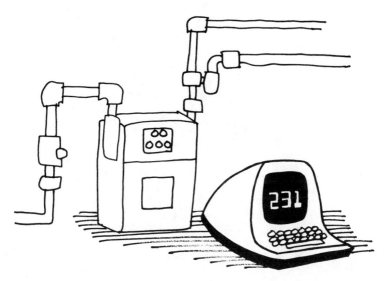

The home controller.

about, talk about, look at, build, and work on. But aside from the inherent pleasures of the personal computer itself, there are many distinct pleasures that can be experienced while using the computer to help out.

Games with Computers

For plain fun and pleasure, personal computers mark the beginning of a new era in home entertainment. Personal computer games like Blackjack, Poker, Star-Trek, and Chess have special features that create intense family involvement. Imagine games that talk, calling each player by their first name. Game "boards" appear in full color on your tv set. "Cards" can be shuffled and dealt. Even keeping score can be handled by your personal computer.

If you have children, a personal computer makes a unique, low-cost babysitter. There are literally thousands of computer games for kids of all ages. These are exciting, educational, and challenging games; the kind kids like the most. There are number guessing games, spelling word games, and games that teach general concepts. You can even create your own games for your children.

You have probably seen the new tv games offered by large de-

Playing games.

partment stores. These are "black boxes" you hook up to your tv, and are nothing more than microcomputers programmed by the manufacturer. With your own computer you can program anything you want, including games like the ones in the stores. When the entire family plays a game, you can have the computer save everyone's score. The computer can retain this information for as long as you wish, giving you the ability to see your skill grow. The best computer games allow the "intelligence" of the computer to be programmed-in. This means you can constantly improve yourself by gradually increasing the skill of your personal computer opponent.

Your Hobby and the Personal Computer

Another interesting facet of the personal computer is that it can usually be integrated into an existing hobby in such a way as to improve the enjoyment derived therefrom. If you are a collector for example (stamps, butterflies, coins, etc.), you can use it to keep track of your collection. When you add to (or remove from) your collection, you can update the computer to reflect the change. Perhaps you are a photographer and have been meaning to get your photographs organized so that you can have quick access to certain ones. This is a perfect opportunity for your personal com-

Organizing your hobby.

puter. One of the things that a computer does best is to keep records in a very organized manner. You can have the computer sort information into any sequence that is meaningful to you.

If you belong to a club that is related to your interests, you will certainly find innumerable ways in which your personal computer would be of use. Most clubs have officers who are elected by the membership. Such an election could be conducted using a personal computer. The balloting could be done in secret, and the votes counted impartially by the computer.

Many clubs send out some sort of newsletter. This means that a list of all of the members in good standing must be kept up to date—an easy job for your club computer. As we have already mentioned, the computer is just great at keeping track of things. And, it can also shuffle things around by name, zip code, or whatever requirement is desired. If you connect your computer to a printer, or maybe to an old teletypewriter machine, you can program it to print mailing labels to speed up the task of sending out the club newsletter.

One other idea related to clubs concerns the organization of various duties and functions that are performed by the club on a regular basis. Things such as benefit luncheons or club-sponsored sports activities could include your club computer as an attraction. The more people that become interested in personal computers, the more interesting they will become. New ideas can be discussed, a sharing of information can take place, and the pleasures of your club will grow.

IN THE OFFICE

Monthly Statements

Perhaps the most practical and profitable use of a personal computer will be in your own small business. For example, instead of spending a whole day or more preparing monthly statements, you can just instruct your personal computer to do it for you. To accomplish this task you just use your computer to keep track of all work that you do for your customers, and also how much each of them pays you. Then, at the end of the month, the computer reports the status of each of your accounts. Besides being able to do this important job for you, your personal computer can also provide you with timely reports pertaining to various aspects of your business. Perhaps the computer can keep track of your appointments throughout the day.

You and any employees whom you might have will be able to know the credit status of any given customer at any given time, as well as how good a customer he really is. If your business involves salesmen calling on your accounts to get business, you can use the computer to analyze their performance. If a product is part of your business, then inventory control is a big part of your business accounting that your personal computer can handle with ease. If you do not have a business now, perhaps your personal computer can be used to aid you in starting a business of your own.

Inexpensive Word Processing

If you have the need to maintain large files of data pertaining to your business, then the computer is an ideal management tool for

In the office.

you. You can use it to help compose letters and documents for your business that will look like they were done by a professional stenographer. If it happens to be a repetitive document such as a listing of items for sale, you can store it all inside your personal computer and quickly update it to reflect current conditions whenever it becomes necessary.

Many businesses require the use of certain forms of documents over and over. Legal forms especially seem to follow the same format although certain information might vary. Your personal computer can provide this kind of flexibility for your business, making it possible to assemble documents using standard formats and internally stored text. In general, anything that you now type or have printed as it goes out of date can be done faster, cheaper, and better with your personal computer.

Job Estimating and Cost Analysis

Knowing how much to charge a customer can often be difficult to determine. If there are many factors affecting the overall nature of the work to be done, the computer can be a real asset to the person in business. If you now spend a significant amount of your productive time just trying to develop a bid on a job, think of how much more profitable it would be to have your personal computer take care of it. The computer can easily keep track of all the minute details of determining the cost of a job, the ones you often overlook. You then spend more time with your customers, and getting the job done. Your customers will see you as a smart business person taking advantage of modern timesaving devices in order to do a better job for them.

When a job is finished, it is sometimes hard to tell if, in fact, it was profitable. How far off was your original estimate of your cost to do the job? Your personal computer can answer these and many other related questions. It can keep track of all the costs and the hours involved in doing a certain job; and upon completion it can give you the details in concise and accurate terms. You can then use this information to help you stay on a profitable track as your business grows. You now have immediate feedback on the results of your business operations and can take corrective action in a timely and efficient manner.

IN THE CLASSROOM

Perhaps the most beneficial use of the personal computer is in education. Because it is versatile, impartial, and patient, the computer can be programmed to assist in the instruction of many different subjects. It can provide real-time interaction between the subject area and the student. For example, after discussion of a certain topic, the computer can ask the student several questions regarding the topic. The student enters his responses to the questions into the computer. Upon analyzing them, the computer will congratulate the student for correct understanding, or reinforce the topic with additional material.

If you are a teacher, and you have to spend many hours just keeping track of grades on quizzes, midterms, and final exams, you could probably make good use of a personal computer. If confidentiality is important, you can program in a secret code so that only you are able to gain access to the information regarding your students.

The computer itself can be quite an educational experience for one who is not familiar with it. Due to its versatility, one of the greatest things it can do is just *be there for someone with an in-*

In the classroom.

quisitive mind to play with. As the student begins to understand what the computer can do, a flood of new ideas will spring forth that might even teach the teacher a thing or two. In fact, unless you're careful, you just might find that you have to wait in line to use *your own computer.*

CHAPTER 4

Programs for Your
Computer

Today, it is difficult to imagine an area of life that remains unaffected by the computer. The hundreds of parts in an automobile are made under control of a computer. The complexity of a television set or a stereo system is made possible by computer circuitry. The telephone, perhaps our most familiar electronic instrument, looks simple from the outside, but the total system that allows us to communicate is actually a formidable array of complex computer circuitry. The computer itself is not really that much more sophisticated than any of these other machines. But, there is one distinct difference that sets the computer apart from the rest—it is programmable.

COMPUTERS ARE PROGRAMMABLE

Because computers are programmable they can be made to act like *many* machines, rather than just one. For example, a toaster is a fixed function machine—it makes toast. It operates according to a rather simple "program," namely:

1. Plug the toaster in,
2. Put bread into the slot(s),
3. Select the desired "brownness,"
4. Push down the lever that activates the toaster.

The toaster does the rest. Now, there are a limited number of variations to this program (the toaster may even throw in one of its own and burn the bread), but it cannot do anything besides make toast.

Even more sophisticated machines like the tv can only do one thing. They are called "fixed function" machines. The tv can only receive and display specially modulated radio-frequency signals. It cannot double as a toaster, or even as a stereo set. Your automobile, although very similar in many ways to an airplane, just will not fly. These cases are true because the "program" that governs the operation of these machines is not available for modification. The computer, on the other hand, is readily reprogrammable at any time. Its program can be completely replaced, or slightly changed in order to achieve some desired goal.

So, just what is a computer program? As we shall learn, there are several parts of a computer that make it what it is. The program is just one of these. There is a microprocessing unit (MPU), a memory, input/output devices, and the program. The program is simply a list of things that the computer has to do in order to complete some objective. In order for the computer to use this list, it must be put into the memory. This can be done in several ways, including typing it in through a keyboard. Once "loaded" into the memory, the program directs the operation of the computer. It is as if the computer is an electronic circuit that is continuously being rewired to make it perform slightly different operations each time.

This rewiring effect is caused by the fact that the actual program, once inside the computer, is reduced to a combination of different voltage levels. This is not, however, the way a human programs a computer. Voltage levels require knowing about power supplies and switching speeds and refresh times, etc. Rather than specifying voltage levels and rewiring plans, what we want to do is to tell the computer in straightforward terms what it is that we want it to do. Then, we can let the computer figure out the voltage levels for itself. We can do this by using a *programming language*. There are several different programming languages in use today, offering a variety of ways to write programs. A programming language consists of several special words and phrases that direct the computer processing. In a sense they do the rewiring. These words and phrases are entered in the computer in the sequence they are to be performed.

These languages are most helpful if you really want to write programs. But what if you just want to use the computer to do a specific thing and don't want to become a programmer? This brings us to one of the first major decision points regarding your computer. Shall you write your own programs, or use programs that someone else has already written?

WRITING YOUR OWN PROGRAMS

Many people get involved with personal computers because they are interested in computers themselves, and are eager to write their own programs. But programming is a very exacting pastime. It requires that *all* things be considered by the programmer with regard to the particular job being done. There are many details that must be attended to so that the finished program will operate correctly. There is a great feeling of satisfaction upon completing a program and seeing it run for the very first time. In fact, programming can be a very creative activity. In programming a computer there are usually several ways to achieve the desired effects. If three programmers were assigned the same job to program, they would probably each do it in a different way. Although there are times when one way is definitely better than another, at other times it really doesn't matter. In order to understand what programming is about let's take a look at a typical program.

Our first example is a program written in BASIC. BASIC stands for *B*eginners' *A*ll-purpose *S*ymbolic *I*nstruction *C*ode. It is probably the most popular programming language used with personal computers. The particular example is a program which simply "reads" in two numbers (A and B), adds them together, calls the sum C, and prints the answer on the output device. We can see that this is accomplished quite readily with only three BASIC "statements."

```
INPUT A,B
LET C=A+B
PRINT C
```

First, to tell the computer to read in data from the keyboard, we use an INPUT statement. It specifies that two numbers are to be read when the user pushes the number keys, and that the numbers will be defined in the computer as "A" and "B." The arithmetic is performed by the LET statement, which is in the form of a simple equation. Finally, to print the answer "C" we only need to tell the computer to PRINT the value of C.

Let's enhance this program a bit and have it communicate with us in sentence form. Suppose we wanted the program to prompt us to enter the two numbers A and B, and also to make the computer print a little message at the end saying, "The answer is C" (stating the value of C). The program would be modified as follows:

```
PRINT "ENTER A AND B"
INPUT A,B
LET C=A+B
PRINT "THE ANSWER IS", C
```

The computer will print out the words "enter A and B" so that we know when to enter them from the keyboard. In less than an eyeblink the computer calculates the answer and prints "the answer is" and the value of C right after it.

For the user very little work or thinking was required to complete this program. That is why BASIC is known as a "high-level language." It does much of the work for you. All that you have to do as the programmer is to enter the program statements in a logical and plain English format. Let's look at another example.

This time, we will program the computer in BASIC to read in five numbers and to print out the largest one. This kind of thing is often done by computers to sort different lists. To find the largest number we will use the ability of the computer to make decisions based upon the data. This is done by using the IF/THEN statement. The program looks like this:

```
PRINT "ENTER FIVE NUMBERS"
INPUT A,B,C,D,E
LET X = 0
IF A>X THEN LET X=A
IF B>X THEN LET X=B
IF C>X THEN LET X=C
IF D>X THEN LET X=D
IF E>X THEN LET X=E
PRINT "THE LARGEST NUMBER IS", X
```

So, to determine which of the five numbers entered is the largest we first start off by making up a test number (X) set to zero. Then, one by one, we compare the five numbers with X. Each time one is found to be greater than (>) X, we replace X with that number. After comparing all five numbers in this way X will be equal to the largest of them all, and will be printed out.

There are many kinds of programs that can be "written" in BASIC language. Since BASIC is mathematically oriented, it is relatively easy to program mathematical operations with numbers and variables. Also, we have seen that in order to get the computer to print out a message, we just enclose the message in quotes within a PRINT statement. If you decide to write your own programs it will most likely be in BASIC, since most of the personal computers available today come with some form of BASIC.

Other high-level programming languages have grown out of the infancy of the computer. In certain application areas like fabrication equipment control, special languages have been developed that better meet the particular needs of that application. In business, also, specialized languages have been developed that are better for large files of customer information than could ever be accomplished by process control. COBOL, a language good for programming business data processing applications on large mainframe systems, has almost become the industry standard business programming language.

FORTRAN is another high-level language that was developed primarily to handle mathematical equation solving with great accuracy. Although it is not a very good language for business applications it has found a home there since it was the only language available for many years. Since those early days of computers, languages like COBOL have become more popular in the business world.

Many microcomputers use programming languages that are very similar to BASIC. Some microcomputers have additional commands that make them even better at handling those large disk files, and outputting long printed reports. Although the computer manufacturers are starting to make available other high-level languages for the personal computers, such as Pascal, FORTRAN, etc., BASIC is the most commonly used language in the personal computer market.

In general, the number and type of different programming languages is as diverse as the number of different computers that are sold today. Every computer manufacturer has some feature on his computer that his competitors don't have on theirs, and vice versa. This is what is so hard to understand for those who don't know computers. If a friend has a program to catalog dead insects using his TRS-80, why can't I just plug that program into my Apple and run it?

Even though the actual program itself may not be "transportable," the programming concepts are. You can convert from one program to another—like BASIC to FORTRAN:

```
      PRINT(3,310)
  310 FORMAT(18HENTER FIVE NUMBERS)
      READ(6,610) A,B,C,D,E
  610 FORMAT(5I3)
      X=0
      IF(A.GT.X) X=A
      IF(B.GT.X) X=B
      IF(C.GT.X) X=C
      IF(D.GT.X) X=D
      IF(E.GT.X) X=E
      PRINT(3,320) X
  320 FORMAT(21HTHE LARGEST NUMBER IS,I3)
```

If you really enjoy getting right down to the fundamentals of computer programming, then you will probably want to learn to program in the "assembly language" for your own particular computer. Assembly languages are much more *symbolic* than BASIC. Rather than instructing the computer in simple English and arithmetic statements, you must use mnemonic symbols that represent each machine instruction to be performed. This type of programming requires that the programmer be intimately familiar with the internal workings of the computer. In some cases, programming in assembly language will involve calculating the time (usually in microseconds) that it will take for each operation to be performed. Usually the programmer will have to deal with *hexadecimal* numbers. Assembly language is generally considered a *lower level* language because the programmer must leave the realm of plain English statements, and arithmetic equations, and enter into the inner logical workings of the computer itself.

Following is a sample assembly language program for a Motorola MC6800 based computer. The sample program moves a block of data from one place in the memory of the computer to another.

Step	Label	Mnemonic	Operand	Description
1		CLR	COUNTER	Clear the counter to zero
2	MOVE	LDAA	AREAA	Load accumulator A with a word from data area A
3		STAA	AREAB	Store accumulator A in a word in data area B
4		INC	COUNTER	Increment the counter by one
5		BEQ	HALT	Branch to HALT if counter became zero
6		INC	LSBA	Increment the OSB of the address for data area A by one
7		BNE	INCB	Branch if not equal to zero to increment area B address
8		INC	MSBA	Increment the MSB of the A area address
9	INCB	INC	LSBB	Increment the LSB of the address for data area B by one
10		BNE	MOVE	Branch if not equal to zero to MOVE another word
11		INC	MSBB	Otherwise, increment MSB of B area address
12		BRA	MOVE	Then branch always to MOVE another word
13	HALT	WAI		This is the HALT for the program

Assembly language programs lend themselves well to such tasks as operating various peripherals connected to the computer. For example, in our sample BASIC program, we told the computer to PRINT several things, but there are many steps involved in getting a computer to print anything on a teletypewriter or printer. Since most of the printing devices used on personal computers print one character at a time, the computer must take care of transmitting the information to be printed, one character at a time. The program must also keep track of how many characters are to be printed, and stop operating the printing device when the last character has been printed. All of these tasks are handled very well by assembly language programs, and the personal computer user who wishes to dabble in these kinds of operations will most assuredly have to become an assembly language programmer.

USING OTHER PROGRAMS

What if you don't have any knowledge of programming, and don't want to learn? Does that mean that you cannot get into personal computing? Absolutely not!

Throughout the world of commercial computing there are thousands of people using computers who do not know the first thing about what makes them tick. These people are termed "users" because they use a computer to allow them to complete some job they are working on. They are using a computer programmed by someone else. Generally, they have requested that the programming be done, and have overseen the development of the program to ensure that it would come out to do what they wanted. Then, they implement the program. If there appears to be some problem with the operation of the program, or if there is some change that they would like to make after using it for a while, they contact the programmer and request that a "fix" be made.

In many cases, the personal computer manufacturers themselves supply various programs (software) with the "hardware" they sell. These are programs that have been written by some programmer for the manufacturer. Since many people want to use computers for similar reasons, it is often possible to acquire "canned programs" for a common application. Sometimes it will be necessary to alter this canned program slightly to accommodate needs of a particular user. This can be done by the manufacturer, but is more often done by the user himself or by some person that the user recruits to change the program. Those who would rather not get involved with programming their personal computer can easily find someone to do it for them.

There are thousands of personal computer enthusiasts belonging to several hundred computer clubs across the country. To save money, the user could contact one of these clubs and ask if there was anyone who might be interested in a little programming job. Without a doubt, there are many people who would jump at the chance to earn a little money helping a user.

The "nonprogramming user" should bear in mind that, for a

given application, once a program is written and "debugged" it should require no further attention. It will work forever as long as the requirements remain the same, and the same computer is used. If it seems to be taking ages for a programmer to finish a particular job, perhaps the job is too difficult, or the programmer is not the best. Before entering into a deal, the personal computer user should get the programmer to commit himself to a specific price for the work, and the estimated time to complete the job. Also, you should arrange for check points at various intervals along the way to see if things are progressing on schedule.

A strange phenomenon associated with computer programmers is that they always seem to be on the move. As new opportunities present themselves, the programmer will almost always shift his life around in order to take advantage of them. This could leave you, the user, high and dry. You might be left with a half-finished program that still requires some finishing touches. Well, you say, why not just take what you have, and find another programmer who can complete the job? This is easier said than done. Assuming that you could find a programmer who would want to take over someone else's work, it would take a long time for this new programmer to figure out what the original programmer was trying to do. As we discussed earlier, there are usually several ways to program the same task, and each programmer will have his own favorite approach. This brings up one very important point concerning *all* programming: All programs should be "documented." This means that there should be a description of what the program is intended to do, how it is supposed to do it, and any special considerations that must be taken in order for the program to work as planned. This is a must if you are planning to have someone else write your programs because the documentation will allow someone else to take over with a minimum of problems, if necessary.

All and all computer programming remains a most interesting subject and will most likely be the center of attention in personal computing for many years. Today, many programmers are of the opinion that the real cost of owning and using a computer will not be in the parts that make it up, but rather in the time and effort that goes into making a working program. It is, therefore, to your advantage to become as familiar as possible with the dynamics of getting a program for your computer that does what you want. It also makes sense to judge a computer not only on its inherent abilities, but also on just what programs the manufacturer has chosen to offer with the computer, how much they cost, and, most importantly, what the future plans of the company are in developing new programs.

There are many software packages available on the market today which have taken many months to develop. They are already documented, and are affordable. But will they work on your computer? For example, the programs in an accounts receivable system are very complicated. There might be a "bug" in one of the programs. This bug might not show itself for quite some time, such as when you try to do the first month-end processing. What happens then? Is there someone that you can call for help? Are you on your own? If you know a little programming, can you figure out what is happening and fix it? Maybe you can't, so your computer is just sitting there on the desk idle.

This may sound like a dismal picture, and it is. Programming is the greatest consideration one should make when shopping for a computer to use in a business. If the machine breaks down, you can just throw it in the back seat of your car and take it down to the computer store to get it fixed. But if the software breaks down you are up a creek without a paddle. If you are not ready to get personally involved with the programs that make the machine work, then be prepared to spend some money getting someone else to do it. As with every other aspect of this microcomputer world, the software will improve in time.

CHAPTER 5

Nuts and Bolts
of a Computer

Perhaps the computers of tomorrow will operate in a way that we have yet to discover. Breakthroughs are being made nearly every day. In the meantime, if we examine the microcomputers of today, we see that, although they are in a different physical form from their full-sized counterparts, much the same design architecture has been employed in both types. This architecture is mainly due to the fact that digital computers operate by using the binary number system, which demands a certain type of logical approach to performing various types of computer operations. We see, therefore, a kind of mimicking of the full-sized computers by this new breed of machine. This leads us to believe that there are some basic concepts about computers in general that can be applied to the microcomputer as well. Of course, there are exceptions to, and variations on, these basic concepts, but generally the processing objectives are the same, and the user of the microcomputers can analyze the different types in order to choose the one best suited for the intended application.

There are five main parts to a computer. These five parts are found, in one form or another, in every digital computer on the market, whether it is the massive system used by an insurance company to keep track of its premiums, or a microcomputer that is used by an individual to control a model railroad. These five main ingredients are:

1. Central processing unit.
2. Memory.
3. Input/output devices.
4. Input/output interfaces.
5. Program.

1. *Central processing unit* (CPU).
   The "brain" of the computer—this is where the actual computing is done. The CPU usually controls all the operations of the computer.
2. *Memory.*
   An electronic storage medium used to hold the program which instructs the CPU and other components of the computer.
3. *Input/output devices.*
   These are the link between man and machine. They vary in type and complexity according to the processing requirements. Input/output devices include keyboards, teletypewriters, video displays, and so on.
4. *Input/output interfaces.*
   These are the "middlemen" between the CPU and the I/O device. They provide the actual hard-wired control of the I/O device, according to the commands that are issued by the CPU.
5. *Program.*
   Without the program, a computer is no more than a handful of parts that sits there and draws current. The program coordinates the operations of the computer in order to perform some desired process.

Each of these five main ingredients will be explored in more detail in this chapter. The emphasis will be on the logical operation of these elements within the computer.

Depending upon the size and intended use of the computer, a sixth part may be added. This is the mass storage device. Its job is to store a lot of computer programs and/or data that is too big to fit into the memory of the computer itself. There are two basic kinds of mass storage in use today, magnetic disk and magnetic tape. Both kinds store the information magnetically, in much the same way that music is recorded on tape. Either type is capable of storing many times the memory capacity of the computer itself.

Both disk and tape are general storage mediums. Information can be stored for awhile, and then erased when it is no longer useful, and the disk or tape can then be used over again for something else. There is a third form of mass storage that is not so flexible. This is read-only memory (ROM) storage, sometimes referred to as "firmware" because it is *firmly* incorporated with the computer and requires some effort to unplug it. Once information has been stored in ROM it cannot easily be changed, lost, or damaged. It is very dependable, has no moving parts, and will save its contents forever.

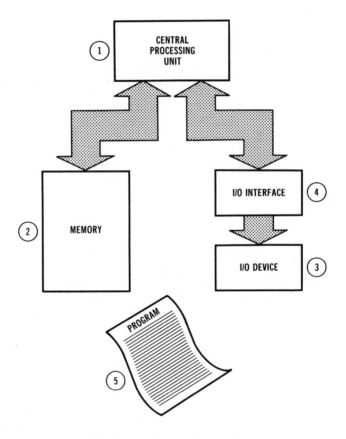

The five main parts to a computer.

CENTRAL PROCESSING UNIT (CPU)

Every computer has some sort of central processing unit (CPU), which is the "brain" of the computing machine. The CPU is a combination of several "parts," interconnected in such a way as to permit certain logical operations to be performed. Computers of 10 years ago required a fairly large enclosure to house the components of their CPUs. Swing-out logic gates holding rows of pc boards, interconnected by garden-hose-sized cable, were not an uncommon sight. Today, the microcomputer uses a CPU that is contained in an LSI chip. This is the *microprocessor*, which, by itself, is not a computer but is the main component in any microcomputer.

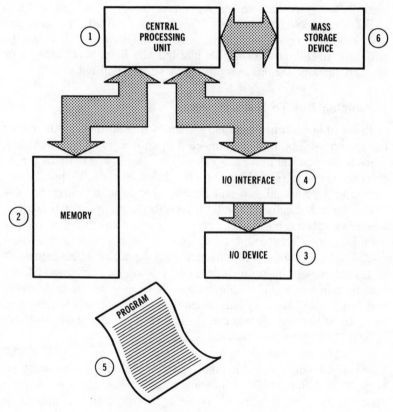

The six main parts to a computer.

Simple Binary Information—the Bit

Microprocessors are digital devices using digital logic concepts to accomplish some processing goal. This digital logic, or binary logic, as it is sometimes called, is based on the fact that certain electronic circuits can be either *on* or *off*, the state being determined by their operating characteristics. These provide a means of defining two "states" or "conditions."

If we have a single circuit, which is to be used to indicate one or the other of two possible conditions, this circuit is said to contain a *bi*nary digi*t*, or *bit* of information. This bit can designate "on" or "off." Another frequent expression is that the bit is a "1" or a "0." This terminology corresponds to the only two numerals in the binary number system. The binary and other number systems are described in further detail in Appendix A.

When we have only one bit, it's plain to see that we can represent only one of two situations. As in the figure, this would be sufficient to tell us whether we had left the front porchlight on or off, but for any serious computing, it simply will not do.

Combining Bits To Make Bytes

To be able to represent more than two conditions with binary logic, several bits may be connected in such a way as to provide a more usable logical unit called the byte. The word "byte" is a contraction of the phrase "binary digit." It has come to be part of the computer jargon and you will hear it used in many different contexts. Byte basically is used to describe a group of 8 bits that, when evaluated together, can represent up to 256 different unique combinations. This could be a number of absolute value from 0–255, or it could be a code that stands for a particular character of the alphabet, including upper- and lower-case characters and punctuation marks. For this reason, it is common to find "byte" and "character" used synonymously. Most computers require one byte to store one character (one letter or one digit 0–9) of information.

So, when you hear someone say that their computer has 32K bytes of memory, you will know that they have the capacity to store 32,000 characters of information. Likewise, when you hear about megabytes, it will usually be in reference to the amount of information that can be stored on some mass storage device. A megabyte is about 1,000,000 bytes or 1,000,000 characters (more exactly it is 1,024,000 bytes).

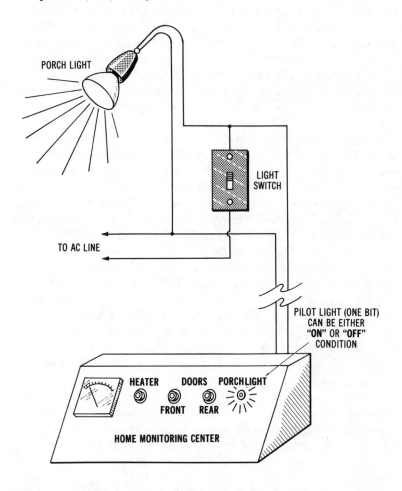

Porchlight circuit yielding one bit of information.

There are other combinations of bits that can be used in a computer and one to expect in the newer machines is 16-bit combinations called "words." As you would think, these larger combinations of bits are capable of storing much larger varieties of information.

Using Bits To Define Instructions

Perhaps the one single attribute that differentiates the microprocessor from other machines is that it can be "told" what to do. This is accomplished by using bytes which contain a bit pattern that is meaningful to the processor. This meaningfulness is determined by the manufacturer. One bit pattern may be used to tell the processor to add two numbers. Another bit pattern may be used to tell it to print a character on a teletypewriter. Another bit pattern may have no meaning to the processor at all.

The group of bit patterns that the manufacturer decides will have some meaning is called the *instruction set*. These instructions will tell the processor what operation it is to perform and, in many cases, how the operation is to be modified due to the bit pattern contained in some other byte. The variety of different operations defined by the instruction set is determined by the manufacturer, in order to fulfill some design criteria. Most instruction sets include some standard arithmetic operations, e.g., addition and subtraction. Also, some "bit manipulation" instructions are usually provided, as well as the frequently used logical operations AND, OR, and EOR (or XOR). Other than these, different instruction sets contain various sorts of operations depending upon the intended application of the processor. Some will be prolific in input/output instructions, if the application demands complicated input or output procedures. Others offer more sophisticated arithmetic instructions in order to process mathematically oriented problems with greater precision.

As shown below, the processor cannot distinguish between bit patterns that are instructions and those that are not instructions. If the processor should accidentally try to execute "data" instead of an instruction, usually an error is created. Some processors contain circuitry that can tell if an invalid instruction is being executed, and will halt the process.

Most processing objectives will require that a certain sequence of steps be performed. For example, suppose that we want to compute the area of a circle using the simple formula

$$\text{area} = \pi \times (\text{radius})^2$$

Since we know that the value of π is a constant, we can rewrite the equation as follows:

$$\text{area} = (3.14) \times (\text{radius})^2$$

Now, suppose that we can somehow "input" the radius of the circle into the computer, and that the computer, after calculating the area, will "output" the answer. The sequence of operations involved here would be:

1. INPUT the radius.
2. SQUARE the radius.
3. MULTIPLY the radius by the value of π.
4. OUTPUT the answer.

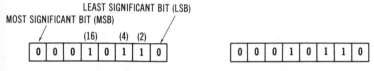

(A) Binary representation of the number 22, in an 8-bit byte.

(B) The bit pattern representing an instruction to add two numbers.

Bit patterns for a data element and for an instruction.

We can appreciate that we would not obtain the correct answer if the operations were not executed in this sequence. For example, if we were to reverse the order of steps 2 and 3, we would be multiplying the radius by the value of π before we squared it, which would yield a totally different answer.

The Instruction Register

Only one instruction can be executed by the processor at any given time. The result of executing one instruction may set up certain conditions that are required for the execution of the next instruction. The sequence of instructions that is to be performed by the processor is usually stored in memory of some kind, which will be discussed in further detail later in this chapter. As each instruction is needed, it is fetched from the memory and put into the instruction register which is a circuit that can electronically hold one instruction.

Electronic circuits in the processor "decode" the instruction and, based on the bit pattern, determine what operation is to be performed. The 1 and 0 bits in the instruction register can be thought

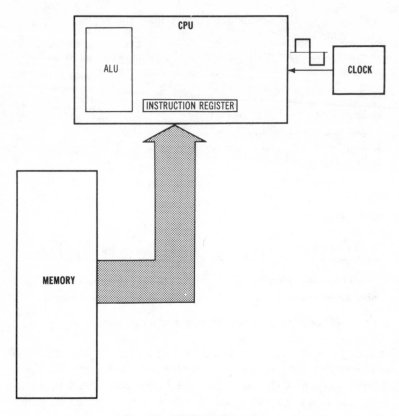

Simplified CPU configuration.

of as "connections," each one being used to shape the circuitry in the processor to enable it to execute the desired operation. The instruction register will contain the instruction all during the time that it is being executed. When it is finished with one instruction, the next instruction in the sequence is fetched from the memory, and loaded into it.

Synchronizing the Operations

We can see that there must be some sort of synchronization of the various operations of the processor. For example, it cannot be fetching an instruction from the memory at the same time that it is executing an instruction already in the instruction register. Also, we must consider that the various operations of the processor will not necessarily require the same amount of time. For example, operations requiring accessing of the memory will take longer to execute than those that do not use the memory. Likewise, operations that involve the activating of some I/O device will initiate some external action of another machine. This may take a million times as much time as is required to execute some instruction that does not use any external I/O device.

For these reasons, there must be a way of getting everything to happen in reference to the same time frame. This can be accomplished in several ways. Some processors use a quartz crystal "clock" to establish a universal time pulse for the coordination of the events that occur internally. Other processors use a simple type of oscillator circuit to provide this periodic signal.

The clock will have a great deal to do with the ultimate speed of the processor, since all the functions are performed in step with the clock. In general, the processor that has the faster clock will perform operations more quickly than the processor that has the slower clock.

We might think of the CPU clock as similar to the crank on the old organ grinder. The faster the crank is turned, the faster the mechanism inside produces the music.

Arithmetic/Logic Unit (ALU)

The arithmetic/logic unit (ALU) is the part of the CPU used to perform the arithmetic and logical operations that are defined by the instruction set. The arithmetic/logic unit contains electronic circuits that perform binary arithmetic as described in Appendix A of this book.

There are various binary arithmetic operations that the ALU circuits can perform. The circuits are directly controlled by a part of the CPU that decodes the instruction in the instruction register and sets up the ALU for the desired function. Most binary arithmetic is based on the "addition" algorithm, or procedure. Subtraction is carried out as a kind of "negative addition." Multiplication and division are generally not performed as discrete instructions, but rather as chains of additions or subtractions under program control. ALUs found in the more powerful microprocessors do offer multiplication and division, as well as other arithmetic operations, in the form of "hardware" circuits which are accessible through one machine instruction.

Arithmetic Modes

There are several types of arithmetic modes used in the microprocessors of today. The most commonly encountered are *signed binary* and *unsigned binary*.

Signed binary arithmetic uses the "leftmost," or most significant, bit (MSB) of the byte to indicate the sign (positive or negative) of the number that is represented by the remainder of the bits. The usual convention here is that, in a negative number, the sign bit will be *set* (equal to 1), and in a positive number, the sign bit will be *cleared* (equal to 0). Generally, negative numbers are stored in a "complemented" form which, as described in Appendix A, makes the binary subtraction operation a negative addition. It is important to note that using one of the bits to indicate the sign of a number reduces the range (or absolute value) of the number that can be stored in the remaining bits. Thus, in 8 bits, using signed binary arithmetic, we can represent numbers from −128 to +127, and of course zero. This is still 256 total different combinations, but even when unsigned numbers are represented, their maximum size is also limited.

The unsigned binary arithmetic mode, as its name implies, does not offer the ability to represent positive and negative numbers. The MSB is *not* used to indicate the sign of the number that is stored. Therefore, the entire byte can be used to store the number. This allows us to store a larger number in each byte but we must be sure that this number will never have to be negative, in order for the operations using it to have some meaning.

The ALU in most microprocessors is capable of handling both these kinds of arithmetic, and of distinguishing between them. Different instructions are used by the CPU to direct the ALU to perform the desired mode of arithmetic. Some microprocessors have ALUs that are capable of doing arithmetic operations on much larger numbers, which may be stored by using more than one byte.

Accumulator and Other Internal Registers

Generally, a number of hardware registers are contained within the CPU. These are used for several purposes by the CPU itself or by the ALU. All microprocessors contain some combination of registers.

The register most commonly associated with the microprocessor is called the *accumulator*. This register is the primary register used during many of the operations that are defined by the instruction set. It is used by the ALU to hold one element of data during an arithmetic operation. It is also directly accessible to the CPU as a working area for many nonarithmetic operations. The accumulator generally has the same number of bits as the defined word length of the particular microprocessor. It is used many times during the execution of a program as the threshold to the memory. The instruction set usually includes some kind of "load" operation, during which the contents of some memory location are loaded into the accumulator. Also, the instruction sets usually include a "store" operation, which causes the contents of the accumulator to be stored at some prescribed memory location.

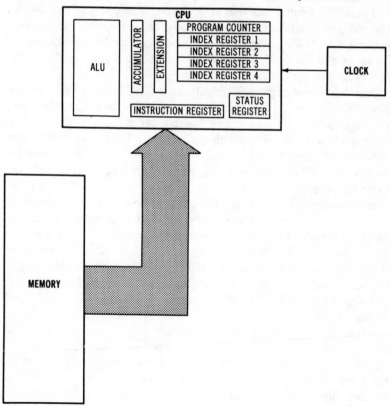

CPU registers.

Probably the next most common internal register found in microprocessors is the *program counter* (PC). This is used to hold the memory location address of the word of memory with which the CPU is concerned at any given time. Each time that an instruction has completed execution, the next instruction must be fetched from the memory. The program counter is used by the CPU to keep track of where in the program the current operation is located. Each time that a new instruction is fetched from the memory, the program counter is modified to contain the memory address of that instruction. The program counter is usually accessible by the program, which means that as a result of processing certain instructions, the PC itself may be changed, thereby forcing the program execution to be taken up at some other point.

The CPU usually has one or more *index registers* available for the storage of information that is going to be used by the program many times. Index registers are also used to hold addresses of areas of the memory that are to be "stepped through," such as tables of numbers.

Another register generally found in a CPU is the *extension register*. The extension register is normally used in conjunction with the accumulator for performing "double-precision" arithmetic. This is an arithmetic mode in which each number is represented by two bytes of memory, both of which must be involved in any operation by the ALU. The extension register is normally used to hold the least significant bits (LSBs) of the number, while the accumulator is used to hold the most significant bits (MSBs) of the number. In this way, the two registers are connected together to form one large arithmetic register. The extension register is also used for other purposes depending upon the manufacturer's objectives in designing the microprocessor. One microprocessor uses this register as a "serial I/O port," where the input data is fed into the extension register's MSB, and the output data is fed out of the LSB of the register.

Another hardware register common to all computers is the *status register*. This is usually a one-word register that is used to keep track of various conditions within the computer. Each bit in the status register word may be assigned a certain meaning by the manufacturer. For example, a certain bit may be "set" if an arithmetic carry occurs as a result of performing some operation in the ALU. A carry occurs when the result of the arithmetic is too large to be represented by the particular word length of the CPU. Another example of the use of this register might be a bit that is used to indicate whether or not some I/O device is requesting service. Perhaps a bit is used by the I/O device to tell the CPU that it has finished the last operation that it was commanded to perform, and is ready to perform the next operation.

Communicating With the CPU

In the previous paragraphs, we have learned about the insides of a typical CPU. We know that CPUs can do various types of arithmetic, that they can interpret certain bit patterns as instructions, and that they have several hardware registers that are used in various ways to aid in the processing. However, the CPU must be given all the information that is pertinent to the operation that is desired. We must furnish the CPU with the instruction and also tell it where to get the data to be operated upon and where to put the result after the operation has been completed. For this purpose, there are communication lines into, and out of, the CPU. These lines are usually a parallel to the binary format that the CPU uses for all of its operations. Therefore, if the word length is eight bits, there will be eight lines connected to the CPU in order to transmit data in or out. This group of lines is called a *bus*, and there are three different types of buses leading into, and out of, the CPU as follows:

1. Data bus.
2. Address bus.
3. Control bus.

We will examine each of these buses individually.

Data Bus — The data bus is used for the transmission of data in or out of the CPU. There are as many lines in this bus as there are bits in the data words for the particular microprocessor. The most common use of the data bus is in transferring information from memory into the CPU, and from the CPU into the memory.

There are some CPUs that have a separate data bus for *reading*, or transferring data from memory to the CPU, and for *writing*, or transferring data from the CPU into the memory. For the most part, this architecture has been avoided since it requires twice as many lines as the read/write combination bus method. In the latter method, the same bus is used for both reading and writing data.

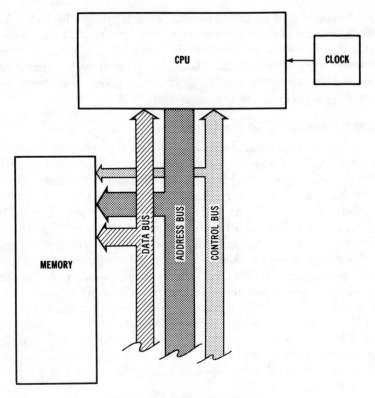

Communicating with the CPU.

Address Bus — This group of lines is used to select the individual location to or from which the transfer of data is to be made. The most common usage of the address bus is in conjunction with the memory. This bus will carry the address of the location in memory that is being accessed by the CPU at any given time.

Some manufacturers have combined the data and address buses into one, shared bus. This is accomplished by multiplexing data and addresses on the same lines. As we might imagine, this requires some sort of synchronization so that, at any time, the CPU can tell whether the bus is carrying data or addresses.

It is also possible to address I/O devices as memory locations. This is done by several microprocessors currently on the market. As long as the I/O device does not interfere with the other uses of the bus, the CPU won't be able to tell the difference.

As we will see in the next section of this chapter, there are many addresses of memory, and perhaps many addresses of I/O devices that need to be represented on the address bus. Therefore, in most processors, we will find that the address bus is wider (greater number of bits) than the word length of the machine.

Control Bus—The control bus is not quite the same kind of group of lines as are the data bus and the address bus. Rather, it is a group of several "dedicated" lines that are each used for some special purpose. Most processors have some sort of a control bus, some more complex and offering more control than others. One of the things that the control bus is used for is to *reset* the processor. This reset function clears the registers in the CPU to all 0's and prepares the processor for the beginning of some program. The reset is normally accomplished by some sort of a front-panel control which is connected to the reset line on the control bus. Likewise, once the processor is operating and actually executing instructions, we would probably desire to have some means to stop everything. Most processors have a separate line that, when switched, causes the processor to stop after completion of the instruction currently being executed.

There are a multitude of other control functions that various manufacturers employ in the design of their processors. Some are used when more than one CPU is to be using the same memory or I/O devices. Others are used to change the CPU operations during execution.

STANDARD BUS STRUCTURE S-100

Since there have been several different types of microcomputers that have been designed by various companies, we would expect that even though they are very much alike, they are also going to differ quite a bit. As with automobiles, we couldn't expect that a carburetor from a Chevy would fit on a Ford. Typically this is true. Although, the very nature of the highly competitive computer marketplace has brought about an interesting twist. Companies are in business today who make "add-on" features that will work on several different computers. This is possible due to the adoption of a standard bus structure called "S-100."

The S-100 bus is so named because it is composed of 100-pin edge connectors, all wired in parallel. It has been agreed upon by the computer manufacturers of today that these 100 pins shall be assigned in a specific manner. Certain pins will be used for the data bus, others for the address bus, and so on. In this way, your computer can be enhanced simply by plugging in a circuit board. The board might contain additional memory, or it might be a special purpose board like a voice synthesizer. The standard bus structure makes a computer much more flexible.

MEMORY

As we have seen in the previous paragraphs, the CPU executes a sequence of instructions, which we call a program, in order to fulfill some processing goal. Since the CPU can deal with only one instruction at any given time, there must be a place to store all of the instructions of the program, and to fetch them, one at a time, for execution. This is the primary use of memory by the computer—to store the program instructions. The memory may also hold data (for example, a constant such as the value of π). In some cases, large tables of data are stored in the memory in order that they may be used as a reference by some program during execution. Whether used for instructions or data, the memory is utilized in the same way for both.

Types of Memory

Although the basic reasons for memory, and the ways that memory is utilized, are the same for both instructions and data, there are several different types of memory, each offering a special feature for the user. We will discuss five of these most common types:

1. *Core*—magnetic core memory.
2. *RAM*—random-access monolithic memory.
3. *ROM*—read-only memory.
4. *PROM*—programmable ROM.
5. *EPROM*—erasable programmable ROM.

Core Memory—Magnetic core memory has been the most popular form of computer memory for quite a few years. This type of memory is known as *nonvolatile* because it will retain the information that is stored in it for an indefinite length of time, and it need not have power applied or be refreshed. Over the years, this form of memory has become reasonably priced. However, the drawbacks of its use with a microprocessor are twofold. First of all, magnetic core does require quite a bit of power in order to write into it. Secondly, its physical size is just not compatible with the LSI technology of microprocessor chips. So, it looks as though the use of magnetic core memory may be waning. At least in the microprocessor fields, the alternatives are much more desirable.

RAM Memory — This memory actually should be called "monolithic random-access memory," but since it has become the most popular type of memory associated with the microprocessor, its name has been shortened simply to RAM. The term *random access* means that any word in the memory may be accessed, without having to go through all the other words to get to it. This memory, being monolithic (that is, being contained in an integrated-circuit chip), is much more suitable to the microprocessor. The power requirement for these memory chips is very similar to that of the microprocessor itself. The signal level necessary to write into this memory is relatively small. The only drawback of RAM memory is that it is a *volatile* form of memory. This means that when the power is removed from the chip, all the memory content is lost. When the power is returned, the content of memory will be unknown. On the other hand, the power consumption of these memory chips is so small that it is feasible to leave them "powered up" all the time. The only eventuality to contend with then would be the occasional power failure or brownout that might cause the loss of the content of memory.

ROM Memory — Read-only memory is very similar to RAM except for one thing. It is not possible to write into ROM memory the way it is to write into RAM. This type of memory is useful, then, only as a source of information, and it cannot be used by the program to store any data or instructions. When purchasing a ROM, the user must specify to the manufacturer exactly what the user wants to be in the memory. The manufacturer, using special equipment, prepares the ROM with the information that the user requests. This information may then be read as many times as desired, and ROM does not require that the power be supplied continuously in order that the information be retained. So ROM memory is also nonvolatile, as is core memory. The ROM memory is useful for such things as the storing of a table of information that is only referred to and never changed. Also, some programs that are required frequently can be stored in ROM and then read into a RAM memory to be executed. Some programs can be executed directly from the ROM, since each instruction is fetched from the memory, and passed on to the CPU instruction decoding logic. If, however, there are any parts of the program that are altered during execution, they cannot be left in the ROM, and they must be read into the RAM memory in order to be executed properly.

PROM Memory—PROM, or programmable ROM, is very much like simple ROM memory, except that it can be programmed by the user in the field. The PROM chips can be purchased blank and then be programmed by using a special machine. Once programmed, this memory behaves the same as the ROM. That is, it can be read as many times as desired but cannot be written into. Also, it is not necessary to supply power continuously to PROM memory in order to preserve the information. In other words, it is nonvolatile memory.

EPROM Memory—This is one of the latest types of monolithic memory. It is called erasable programmable ROM. It can be programmed in the field by the user, and it can also be erased and reprogrammed with different information. Once it has been programmed, the EPROM memory acts just the same as ROM. Again, this is a memory that cannot be written into, but it can be read as many times as necessary.

One way of combining memory types is shown in the block diagram on the next page.

Organization and Addressing of Memory

In organizing and addressing memory, the first fact that we should remember is that memory for a digital computer will have to be in binary form, because all information in a digital computer is stored in binary. Second, we must remember that each microprocessor has a word length that is determined by the manufacturer. This word length is the number of binary "bits" that are grouped together into one logical unit of information in binary. From these two facts, we can see that memory must be able to store information in binary words of the same length as the microprocessor word.

All types of memory that were described in the last section are constructed so that they fulfill the requirements of binary memory. They are subdivided into words, each of which contains a bit pat-

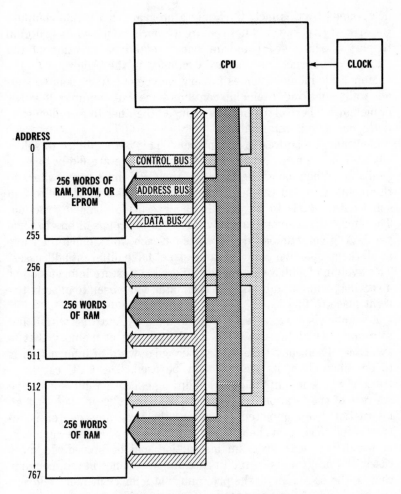

Combining RAM and ROM memories.

tern representing an instruction in the program or perhaps data which is to be operated upon by the computer program.

The next question is: How much memory is needed by the computer? This is a totally variable number which is dependent on several conditions. The complexity of the application for which the computer is going to be used is the first criterion for determining how much memory is needed. If there is going to be a need to store large amounts of data in memory, then the requirements may be determined by this fact. Certainly a program that would compute the area of circles would not require as much memory as a program to play chess, since program size is mainly a function of the number of instructions that are contained in the program.

Monolithic memory comes in very convenient IC packages, and, generally speaking, each chip contains some fixed number of words of memory. These chips may be grouped together to form however much memory is required.

Consider the addressing of memory. This is the ability to select any one of the many words of memory that we are likely to have available. When using the memory, the CPU must know where in the memory to find the next instruction, or possibly where to find some data that is to be used in the execution of an instruction. Therefore, the memory (already arranged in groups of bits to form words) is given numbered addresses for each word, much the same as all the people living on the same street have different addresses. This system of addressing makes it possible to store information at a specific memory address, and then later come back to exactly the right place to find it.

A number is assigned each word in memory, starting with 0 and continuing as high as need be for the amount of memory that is available. Then, any time that a particular word of information is to be referred to, its address may be used. The CPU can keep track of where it is in the program during execution, by storing the address of the location in the program counter. Each time that an instruction has completed execution, the program counter is incremented to contain the address of the next word in the memory, in which the next program instruction will be stored. In most cases, the program is stored in ascending sequence in the memory; that is, the beginning of the program is at a lower memory address than the end of the program.

Reading From Memory

Reading from memory is the act of getting the information that is stored in the memory out of the memory and putting it into some other place where it can be used. This is why earlier in this chapter we referred to this process as "loading" the contents of a memory location into a register. The contents of the memory location are not changed by the operation of reading from that memory location.

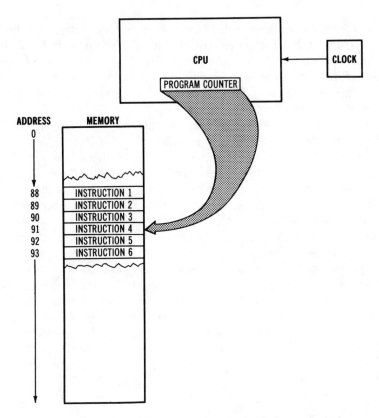

Program counter "points" to the instruction being executed.

Writing Into Memory

Writing into memory is the process of putting some information into the memory for storage. Earlier in this chapter, we referred to this process as "storing" the contents of a register into a memory location. Of course, the writing process destroys the previous contents of the memory location and replaces them with the new information. This writing cannot be done with ROM memory, since there are no circuits in the ROM chip to receive the information.

INPUT/OUTPUT DEVICES

In this chapter about basic computer concepts, we started at the center with the CPU and worked our way to the "outside world."

For it is in the outside world that the ultimate effect of the processing inside the computer will be felt. The computer's function will have significance for whoever will use this powerful instrument. Since humans are not equipped with address and data buses that can be connected directly to the computer, we must have some other way of communicating with it.

Many forms of information may be entered into the computer. Depending upon the application and the volume of information that is likely to be involved, there are several machines that can be connected to a computer. These machines are constructed so that they can be operated by humans. The machine translates the operations into signals that can be interpreted by the computer. Some of these devices translate the signals generated by the computer into a "human language." These machines are called *input/output devices*, or more simply, *I/O devices*.

It is not always necessary that the computer be connected to some "human" interface. In many applications, the computer is used as a controller of other machines. Some applications involve several computers communicating with each other. In all cases, however, some kind of an interface with the world is necessary. It may be as simple as two wires used to turn something on and off, or it may be as complex as several dozen video monitors giving flight information to passengers at the airport.

Data Terminal

The most commonly encountered form of the I/O device is the data terminal. This is actually a combination of an input device and an output device in one convenient cabinet. The input device takes the form of a keyboard that is very similar to that of a typewriter. The output device is a screen just like a television, on which various types of information can be displayed. These two devices can be combined in a number of ways. Both devices can be contained in the same enclosure. This is the true "terminal" that is a familiar sight around any large computer system. A terminal itself is not necessarily a computer (but often it contains a computer chip to make it work). There may be many of these terminals connected to one computer system. They allow information to be *input* to the system via the keyboard, and *output* from the system onto the tv-like screen. The keyboard part of the terminal consists of an arrangement of electronic key switches, that when pressed gener-

Data terminal.

ate a binary code that represents the character. This code is called ASCII and stands for American Standard Code for Information Interchange. The name is pronounced "ass-key," and the code consists of eight bits of information. With these eight bits, all of the characters of the alphabet (both upper and lower case), the numerals, the punctuation marks, and some special characters can be represented. A keyboard that has been removed from the enclosure is shown below. As you can see, the key switches are mounted right on a circuit board which also contains some electronic components that produce the ASCII codes. These codes can then be sent to the computer system data bus as input. They are then interpreted by the computer and dealt with as required.

The output part of the data terminal operates much the same as a standard television. In fact, many times a tv can be used as a "video output" device. The terminal contains a crt (cathode ray tube) just like a tv. But, instead of displaying picture information on the screen, it displays information in the form of characters and numbers arranged in some meaningful layout. A typical screen layout for data processing purposes is shown below. Graphic data

Courtesy Stackpole Components Co.

ASCII keyboard.

can also be displayed, even with color added to provide additional meaning.

There are some terminals available today that specialize in the use of color graphics. These can be used to provide complex interpretations of statistical information, circuit designs, navigational coordinates, survey maps, and many other things.

Some personal computers have both the keyboard and video display devices built right into the cabinet. This makes the whole computer a "stand-alone" device which does not require any other devices in order to work. Other computers have the keyboard built in, but require an external video output device. This can be in the form of a video monitor, or in many cases a standard tv. If a tv is used as an output device, then there will have to be an interface device known as a video modulator between the computer and the tv. The purpose of this modulator is to convert the video signal from the computer to the same frequency as regular tv broadcasts.

Depending on the intended use of the terminal, some terminals will have additional keys. There are some terminals that have the familiar 10-key adding machine configuration to facilitate numeric entry. Other terminals that are specialized for word processing will have special function keys, such as "delete sentence" and "move block," which will invoke certain text editing processes. Of course, terminals that are intended for use with color graphics may have

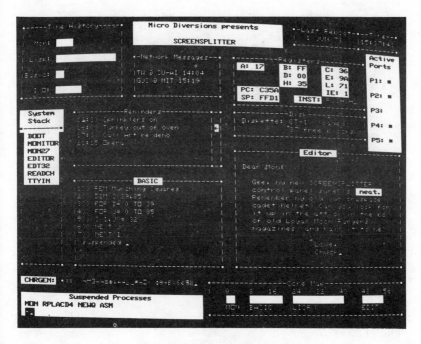

Typical screen layout.

still more special function keys to control the output of the graphics information.

Printers

While in many cases the data terminal will be all the I/O that a computer needs, often it is necessary to preserve the output for later use. This is called "hard-copy" and requires some sort of printing device. There are several popular types of printing devices available today, probably the most common is the standard "impact printer." These printers operate much the same as a typewriter. Paper is fed through a platen, there is an inked ribbon, and character impressions are created by impacting the ribbon against the paper. Again, this can be done in several ways. The most common impact printer is known as a matrix printer because it creates the images in the form of a matrix of dots.

A typical matrix printer is shown below. Here again, the ASCII code is used to represent the characters inside the computer. This

Standard tv used for video output device.

Courtesy Axiom Corp.

Typical matrix printer.

code is sent to the printer over wires. Once the code arrives in the printer, it controls a group of solenoid operated pins that strike the ribbon against the paper in a pattern of dots that forms the character.

There are other types of impact printers including the "character printer," sometimes called "daisy-wheel" printer. This is because, instead of using a pattern of dots to form the image of the characters, the printer contains a mechanically operated type element. This is usually in the form of a round wheel that has many flexible fingers protruding out from it. On each finger is the raised image of one character. When the ASCII codes for the characters are sent to the printer, the wheel is made to turn to the proper position for printing each of the characters that has been sent. When the proper character finger is in position, a solenoid drives the finger against the ribbon, thereby printing the character on the paper.

Most of these printers are pretty fast compared to a typewriter. The matrix printers generally have a speed of about 150 characters per second, while the daisy-wheel printers print at about 60 characters per second. To equate this to typing speed, consider every five characters as one word. This means that the matrix printer can print at a rate of 30 words per second, or 1800 words per minute. While this may seem very fast compared to typing speed, there are other printers known as "line printers" that can print even faster. They print so fast that their speed is no longer referred to in terms of characters per second, but rather in lines per minute. They are called line printers because they generally print a whole line at a time.

Other I/O Devices

There are many other types of I/O devices that can be connected to a computer. Most of these devices are in conjunction with some special application. There are game related I/O devices like paddle controls and joysticks for flying imaginary starships. There are buttons used for firing laser weapons and photon torpedos. Some computers have voice synthesizers which have a stored vocabulary for communicating with the user. There are music synthesizers which can be programmed to play Bach fuges, or punk rock. In general, the more elaborate the computer application, the more elaborate I/O devices are associated with it.

INPUT/OUTPUT INTERFACES

In the previous section, we have discussed various kinds of I/O devices. We have seen that these are the interface between man and machine. These I/O devices, however, cannot simply be "plugged in" to the computer and be expected to work. There is a significant amount of interfacing that must be done between machine and machine. One kind of interface is shown below.

Control Lines

One of the most essential parts of I/O interfacing is that of controlling the device. For example, if we are using a magnetic-tape storage device with the computer, we will want to be able to start and stop the tape transport mechanism at will, usually under control of the program. In general, control lines are used to operate a mechanical device, at the will of the program.

I/O interface for cassette tape.

Status Lines

Closely associated with the control lines, these lines are used so that the computer can determine the condition of an I/O device. This is necessary, for example, if the program is ready to issue a command to the printer to print a character, and the machine is still in the process of printing the previous character. A status line will tell the computer that the printer is busy and is not ready to receive the next character yet. When the printing operation is completed, the status line will indicate to the computer that the printer is ready to perform the next operation.

Another example of the use of a status line is in the operation of the ASCII keyboard. When a key is depressed, a status line will indicate to the computer that someone has pressed the key and that there is information ready to be entered. Sometimes another line is used to tell the computer that more than one key is being pressed at the moment, and to ignore the data.

Data Lines and Buffers

Of course, there must be some means of actually getting the information into, or out of, the computer. This is the purpose of the data lines. In most cases, the processor's data bus is used for this purpose. Some processors treat I/O functions as though they were simply references to memory.

Usually the computer has a limited ability to send and receive information on the data lines. In this case, the I/O interface must also contain circuitry that can buffer or temporarily store the information sent from the computer so that it can be modified in some way to make it usable by the device.

Synchronizing and Timing

When some types of I/O devices are used, the transfer of information between the computer and the device must take place under very close timing specifications. This is especially true for devices that communicate with the computer by using only two wires. These are called *serial* devices, since they send, or receive, information as a string of bits. The bits are sent one after the other at a very precise rate. This mode of transmission is useful when the I/O device is a long distance from the processor, and telephone lines are used to connect them. However, when the distance between the device and the computer is relatively short, the information can be transmitted as a complete word of data; all the bits in the word are sent simultaneously, with several wires being used to facilitate the transfer. This is called *parallel* I/O, because all the bits are transferred on several parallel lines simultaneously. An example of a parallel I/O device is the ASCII keyboard. When a key is pressed, the electronic circuitry associated with the keyboard interface generates the proper bit pattern for the character selected and puts it into a buffer as one word of binary data. The computer must then be notified that a key has been pressed and that there is a word of data in the buffer. Then, under the

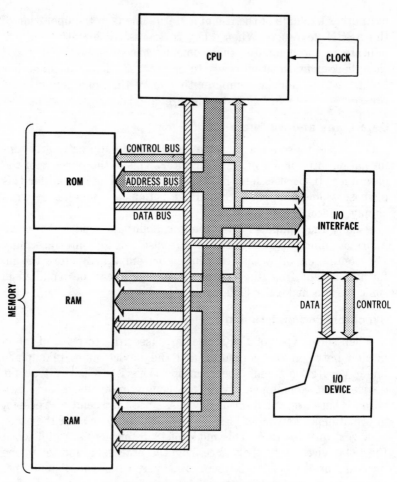

I/O on the processor's buses.

control of the program, the computer will read the word from the buffer and proceed to process it.

We can see that, in this case, there is very little need for synchronizing and timing, as compared with the previous examples of serial devices.

Interrupt Processing

As was discussed, there are many times when it is necessary to communicate with the computer, and each one of these cases requires the attention of the computer at some time or other in order to accomplish the transfer of information. In almost all cases, the information must be transferred under the control of the program. This would lead us to believe that the computer would always be tied up trying to determine if some device was trying to send or receive information. This would be the case if it were not for the ability of almost every microprocessor to be very carefully interrupted.

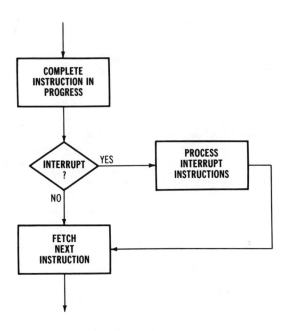

Flowchart for interrupt processing.

One of the control lines leading into the CPU is used to interrupt the normal flow of the program being executed. When a signal is put on this line, the CPU will complete the particular instruction being executed. It will then be forced into a special section of the program which will make a note of the place where the interruption occurred and will analyze the various conditions of the system to determine what caused the interrupt. In this way, the computer can be working on some part of the program, and will process I/O only when the need arises and when a device causes an interrupt in the processing.

Direct Memory Access (DMA)

Most I/O devices require the attention of the CPU in order to communicate with the memory. For instance, if there is some information in the memory that we wish to be printed on the printer, the program must take care of transmitting every character to the I/O device. This will require many instructions each time a character is printed.

A *direct memory access* (DMA) device, on the other hand, is one that can communicate with the memory of the computer without having to go through the CPU. This means that the I/O interface for this device must be capable of generating memory addresses, as well as providing the data transfer. These devices usually use the system address and data buses, just as the CPU itself does. As discussed in the section on the CPU, these buses are greatly used by the CPU, and if they are to be used by other parts of the system, there must be provision for control of the bus. Therefore, the DMA device interface must also be able to share the buses with the CPU and to coordinate their use.

MASS STORAGE DEVICES

Every operation that a computer does requires some form of memory. Program instructions are stored in the "main memory" of the computer, where they are available for immediate execution. Some data that is to be used in the operation of the computer may also be stored in main memory. Main memory is also known as "high-speed" memory, since it is usually composed of solid-state memory chips. While this memory may be fast, its cost keeps the total storage capacity of any computer small. Most personal computers contain about 32K bytes of main memory. This is just right for the execution of a fairly complex program. But, what if you want to use several different programs at different times. On Monday, you want your computer to be a bookkeeper, and on Wednesday, you want it to help you solve differential equations. The main memory of your computer is not large enough to contain both of the programs that you want to use. It can hold one, or the other.

Floppy Disk

What you need is a "mass storage" device. This is sometimes called secondary memory. It generally takes the form of a magnetic disk storage device. This device, more commonly called the "disk," is made like a 45 rpm record. Because it is made from a flexible mylar material, it is called a "floppy disk." Information can be stored on the surface of this disk magnetically, as is done with music on recording tape. This means that you can store programs that you are not using at the moment on a disk, and then when you need to use it, just read it into the main memory from the disk. Data files can also be stored on the disk for use at some later time.

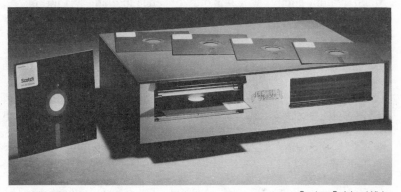

Courtesy Peripheral Vision

Floppy disk mass storage device.

A "dual floppy" disk drive unit capable of utilizing two floppy disks at the same time is shown below. The actual floppy disk is round. It is inside a stiff cardboard jacket which is square, and has a hole in the middle for the drive spindle, and another hole in the form of a slot which runs along the radius line of the disk. When the disk is inserted into a disk drive unit, the large round hole in the center rests on a rotating spindle. This makes the disk rotate just like a record on a record player. Since the information is recorded on the disk magnetically, there are many "tracks" on the disk which are "read" and "written" by a recording head that moves back and forth inside the slotted hole. The tracks may be thought of as a group of concentric circles, getting smaller as they approach the center. The head mechanism can position itself over

97

any one of the tracks just by moving a small amount. This is why floppy disks are called "random access" devices. Unlike magnetic tape which we will discuss later in this section, the floppy disk drive does not have to search through the whole tape to find a particular program or data file. This means that the floppy disk is a fairly fast form of secondary memory. The average "seek time" of a floppy disk drive is 0.3 second. This is the average time it takes to move the head mechanism from any point on the disk to any other point.

The first logical question about floppy disks is "How much information can be stored on a floppy disk?" A typical floppy disk layout using an 8-inch disk is shown below. There is also a smaller disk called a "mini-floppy" which is only 5 inches in diameter. Of course, this smaller disk cannot hold as much information as the larger one, but the method of figuring its capacity is the same.

This disk that we are looking at has 77 tracks, in the form of concentric circles around the spindle hole. You might think that the tracks closer to the center would not hold as much information. They do because the whole disk turns at some fixed number of revolutions per minute, usually 300 rpm. When data is written (recorded) on the disk, a constant stream of bits is sent to the head. In this manner, there is always the same number of bits written with each revolution of the disk regardless of which track is being written.

Each track is further divided into 26 sectors. These can be thought of as if the disk was a pie that was cut into 26 pieces. The reason for this sector idea is mainly to provide more structure to the disk layout so that the disk drive mechanism can deal with parts of a given track without having to deal with the rest of it. Each sector contains 128 bytes of information. Remember that a byte is equivalent to a "character" in most computer systems. This means that 128 characters of information can be stored in each sector on the disk. So now we can figure out the total capacity:

$$
\begin{array}{rl}
128 & \text{bytes per sector} \\
26 & \text{sectors per track} \\
77 & \text{tracks per disk} \\
\hline
= 256{,}256 & \text{bytes per disk}
\end{array}
$$

While there are other disk formats that contain more information, this example is typical of many of the formats that are being used

and is called the IBM 3470 format. (More specifically, this is the
IBM 3470 single-density, single-sided 8-inch standard.)

SINGLE DENSITY
256 K byte
8″ Diskette
FM encoded 3408 bits/in
77 tracks
26 sectors/track
128 data bytes/sector
2002 total sectors
74 data tracks
2 bad track reserves
1 maintenance track

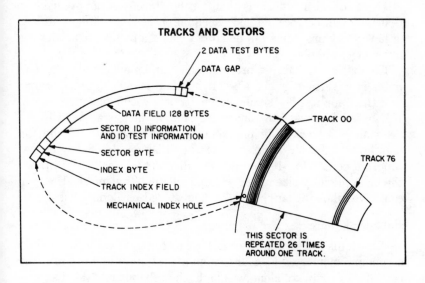

IBM 3470 floppy disk single density format.

So, the 8-inch floppy disk contains about ¼ million characters of
information storage. In computer jargon we would say 256K. Just
how much storage is 256K? Let's look at a typical example involv-

ing the use of a floppy disk to store a file of names and addresses of the members of a club. The following information shall be stored:

Member Name	36 characters
Address	35 characters
City	35 characters
State	2 characters
Zip code	9 characters
Area code	3 characters
Telephone	8 characters
Total	128 characters

So, it would require 128 bytes of storage for each member. Dividing 256,256 bytes per disk by 128 bytes per member equals 2002 members per disk (one member per sector—nice).

The foregoing example is not meant to imply that a single floppy disk system is *all* that you would need to implement a club membership system of 2000 members. It is only meant to be an illustration of the capacity of an 8-inch floppy disk.

There are also programs that can be stored on floppy disks so that they can be recalled and executed on demand. To get an idea of how many programs can be stored on a floppy disk, consider the following example.

The size of the largest program that can be executed on a computer is governed by the size of the main memory. Let's assume that the computer is a small personal model with a main memory of 16K bytes. That is, 16K binary (16×1024) which is actually 16,384 decimal. So, how many programs of that size would fit on the floppy disk? Divide 256,256 bytes per disk by 16,384 bytes per program equals 15.64 programs per disk. This is at least 15 times the main memory size in our example of 16K. That means that you can have whole libraries of programs stored on floppy disks.

Hard Disk

Floppy disk has been the most cost effective way of providing secondary memory for small computer systems. While at first the cost of the hardware alone was high, the reliability of the disk systems was low. Things have come a long way, and we are now experiencing the beginning of floppy disk systems. The technology has improved greatly, and the cost of the media (the floppy disk itself) is low.

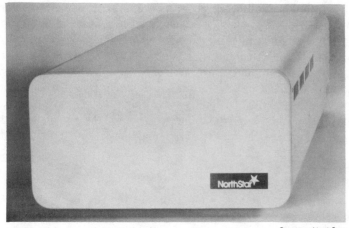

Hard disk drive.

There are some drawbacks to using floppy disk systems. One of them is that the disks wear out, and must eventually be replaced. This means that if there are any programs or data files that you will want to keep for a long time, you must continuously make "back-up" copies of them on another floppy disk that is saved. Eventually, this back-up disk will become worn out from making regular copies, and so there must be a "back-up of the back-up," and so on.

While the drawbacks are there, they are usually insignificant when compared with the convenience and power of the floppy disk systems. There is even newer technology in the making. Until now "hard disk" systems were just too expensive for the small computer user. The hard disk is basically the same concept as the floppy disk except that it isn't floppy. Instead of mylar, it is made of solid aluminum in the shape of a disk that is coated with magnetic recording material. The hard disk, and the read/write head are enclosed in a plastic covering that is air-tight. No contamination can get to the disk, which means that it will not wear out as fast. The disks can be formatted much denser in order to provide storage capacity of about 5 megabytes on a 5-inch hard disk.

This type of mass storage device could easily be built right into the cabinet of a small computer. There would always be 5,000,000 bytes of secondary storage attached to the system. This would be enough for a lot of different programs, as well as some fairly large data files. This type of system could also contain another mass storage device for communicating with the rest of the world. Since the disk is sealed, it cannot be exchanged with another disk as the floppy systems can. Therefore, the only way to put anything onto the disk (besides typing it from the keyboard) is through some alternate storage media. Before long there will be systems with the built-in hard disk, and one floppy drive for the alternate media. Another alternate media could be magnetic tape, which is discussed in the next section.

Magnetic Tape

Magnetic tape is a storage medium that consists of the same kind of magnetic tape as that used for the recording of audio signals by a tape recorder. There are several different sizes of tape which are used for this purpose. The most common magnetic tape format used with microcomputers is the familiar cassette cartridge.

The basic idea here is the same as that in the recording of music, except that instead of music we are recording binary information (1's and 0's) in a magnetic format that can later be read to re-create the binary information and feed it back into the computer. Although the cassette storage devices are quite a bit more sophisticated than the regular garden-variety cassette recorders, they are also more expensive. Many microcomputer systems operate quite well using a $20.00 cassette tape recorder as an I/O device. This provides a convenient medium for storing programs and data without spending a fortune.

An important thing to remember about magnetic tape is that, due to the fact that the tape is wound onto reels, the information is available only in a sequential manner. That is, if the desired information is somewhere near the end of the tape, the machine must read through all the information that precedes it on the tape, until the sought-after information is found. There is no way that the machine can go directly to the information.

SOFTWARE

One fact that cannot be overstressed is that, regardless of the complexity of the various electronic devices that the computer comprises, the computer is nothing more than an expensive toy

Magnetic tape drive.

Courtesy Panasonic

Cassette tape recorder mass storage device.

unless there is a purpose for its existence and a program that will cause the purpose to be realized. It is the program, consisting of the individual instructions arranged in the order that they are to be performed, that will make the computer a useful tool to many.

There are many different types of programs and programming systems, all of which are referred to as *software*, as opposed to the electronic and mechanical elements of the computer, or the *hardware*. Some of these programs are used to accomplish a particular computing goal, such as to balance a checkbook or compute the area of circles. Other programs are used to operate the many I/O devices that we have discussed. The mechanical operation, as well as the transfer of the information between the computer and the device, is controlled directly by the program. Still other programs are used for special-purpose types of computing, for example, computing the square root of a number or doing any other arithmetic that the hardware (ALU) does not do itself. Sometimes these types of programs are referred to as *subroutines* because they are usually part of some larger program. For some given computer system, many programs may be collected, and all stored on magnetic disk. Then, one program is used to selectively "call in" any of these many programs that are to be used. Such a collection of programs is called an *operating system*, and if it happens to be stored on a magnetic disk, it is called a *disk operating system*.

Start-up Programs

The first consideration for the new computer user will be, "How do I get this thing to start?" Just applying the power to the computer will not cause it to immediately begin processing in the way that the user desires. There must be a program that initializes the system and then determines what the user's processing goals are. Once this is established, there must be a program that will set up the computer to perform the desired processing. A most convenient method of accomplishing this "start-up" is to have a program such as that described here, stored in read-only memory (ROM), which will automatically be executed when the computer is turned on.

Writing Programs

There are many ways to program a computer. But, before you sit down and begin, you should always make a thorough evaluation of just what it is that you want the computer to do. Once this step has been done, you can then embark on your programming mission. Perhaps you want the computer to activate a loudspeaker, creating sounds as part of a computer game. This kind of task is probably best handled by a small "machine language" program that can be "called" by the game program when a sound is necessary. On the other hand, if you want the computer to balance your checkbook, machine language will not be a very good approach.

Most microcomputers that are available today include a package of programs known as an "operating system." This package usually includes features that allow the computer to be programmed using one of the "high-level" programming languages. These languages incorporate powerful commands like "PRINT" which causes the computer to output something, and "INPUT" which does the obvious opposite. With these kinds of high-level programming languages, it is quite easy to write programs to balance your checkbook, or to take care of inventory control problems, and the like.

Buying Programs

With the tremendous impact of the microcomputer on the consumer market, there have been many companies that have sprung up which provide various kinds of "canned programs" for the general application areas. There is a myriad of game programs that will operate on many different kinds of computers. Some of these are available on cassette tape at a relatively low cost. These are programs that some programmer has written and tested and then "dumped" onto the cassette in a standard form so that other computers, equipped with cassette tape I/O, can easily read them and run them.

There are also several software companies that are developing general business systems that will operate on a microcomputer. These are usually available on a floppy disk since they are generally much more complicated than the game programs. There are general ledger programs, accounts receivable programs, inventory control programs, to name but a few. Most of these come complete with operating instructions, and sample reports. These are very useful programs for small businesses that have never used a computer before and, therefore, do not have prejudices about how the system is supposed to work. If a company has had any previous experience with a computerized accounting system, then there will probably have to be some "modifications" made to the programs in the canned system.

CHAPTER 6

30 Computers Compared

Now that you have a better idea of how a computer functions as a multipurpose machine, you are ready to take a look at real personal computer products on the market. This chapter is a mini-catalog of 30 different personal and small business computer products, examined in the light of what these authors consider important.

To make things easy, the products are listed alphabetically by name and model number. The architecture is stated as one of the three we described in the hardware chapter—handheld, desktop, or mainframe. The microprocessor that is installed in the computer is also given. The maximum memory capacity and price is given as well as the standard mass storage device that comes with the base unit—cassette recorder, floppy disk, or plug in ROM pack. The price with minimum and maximum memory is given.

We describe the display characteristics in enough detail to allow you to understand the best resolution and graphics effects attainable. Also covered is the number of colors available and built-in sound making capability if any. The computer's expandability (kind of bus, ease of interfacing, buffering, interrupts, etc.) is listed so you can get an idea of what is involved in adding peripherals. The software media that the computer is capable of using is given. Special features of the computer (such as unique graphics statements, hefty power supply, etc.) are listed for each computer. Finally a comments section gives the author/reviewer's *subjective* impression of the product.

This section is by no means to be considered the final word on any product listed here or sold today. Rather, this data is provided primarily to give the reader a general overview of the market, and to prepare or "prime" one for the eventual "trip to the store." Just like when buying a car, it is always a good idea to read a consumer report on the car you are interested in *before* you buy it.

It is important to note that minimum price usually, but not always, implies minimum memory. In this book the "base" price is the price of the unit with either 16K or less of RAM. In most cases we have given the price for a 16K configuration, even if a smaller size is available. The reason for this is that the greatest number of high quality and practical programs are over 16K bytes in length. Therefore, because the smaller size machines will suffer from this deficiency, we give the 16K prices when possible so as to keep the comparisons more equal. Since 16K of RAM cost less than $50.00 today, it makes sense to go for 16K immediately. Some computers have a maximum of 2K memory (the Tandy Pocket computer and Sinclair ZX-80). The prices listed are those supplied at the time of writing (early 1981) and are given for comparison purposes only. It should be noted that prices may vary between dealers and are subject to change.

The computer products in this chapter are arranged alphabetically by name of the company that manufactures or distributes the product as follows:

APF Imagination Machine IM-1
Apple II
Apple III
Atari 400
Atari 800
Commodore PET 4000 Series
Commodore CBM 8000 Series
Cromemco System Three
Cromemco Z2-H
Cromemco System Zero
Dynabyte 8/2
Exidy Sorcerer
Heath H-8
Heath H-11
Heath H-89

Hewlett Packard HP-85
ISC Compucolor II
ISC Intercolor 8000 Series
Mattel Intellivision
NorthStar Horizon
Ohio Scientific Superboard
Radio Shack TRS-80 Color Computer
Radio Shack TRS-80 Pocket Computer
Radio Shack TRS-80 Model III
Radio Shack TRS-80 Model II
Radio Shack TRS-80 Model I
Sinclair ZX-80
Texas Instrument TI-99/4
Vector Graphics
Zenith Z-89

APF IMAGINATION MACHINE IM-1

Name and Model Number	APF Imagination Machine IM-1.
Manufacturer's Name and Address	APF Electronics, Inc., New York, NY 10036.
Architecture	Desktop with 6800 microprocessor.
Maximum RAM Memory Capacity	9K bytes.
Mass Storage Device With Base Unit	Cassette recorder built-in with parallel data and voice tracks, and computer motor control.
Price with Base RAM	$599 (1K).

APF IMAGINATION MACHINE IM-1
(Continued)

Price with Maximum RAM	$899.95 requires building block BB-1 expansion connector ($199.95) plus 8K RAM module ($99.95).
Display Type	Color or black and white television, modulator built-in for Channel 3 or 4.
Screen Format	Text: 32 columns by 16 lines with three color characters. Graphics: low resolution graphics plus text—64 horizontal elements by 32 vertical elements in 8 colors, high resolution 1, 128h by 192v, high resolution 2, 256 by 192v.
Number of Colors	Pure text mode—2 colors. Text plus graphics mode—8 colors. Highest resolution allows two colors and two color sets to select from.
Sound Capability	Built-in speaker with volume control. BASIC language statement called MUSIC followed by parameters allows easy programming of sound effects and tunes.
Expandability	Requires an additional "building block" unit to expand, has room for extra RAM modules.
Software Media	Cassette, mini-disk, plug-in ROM cartridges.
Special Features	Two built-in game control units house joystick, 12 calculator keys, and a "fire" key. BASIC graphics statements COLOR, SHAPE, PLOT, HLIN, VLIN similar to Apple.

APF IMAGINATION MACHINE IM-1
(Continued)

Comments   A truly innovative product, the APF Imagination machine contains a 6847 LSI graphics chip (see Computer Graphics Primer, Howard W. Sams & Co., Inc., catalog number 21650 for details on this part). There are certain limitations on expanding the IM-1. An excellent user manual and newsletter is provided.

APPLE II AND APPLE II PLUS

Name and Model Number	Apple II™ and Apple II Plus™.
Manufacturer's Name and Address	Apple Computer Inc., 10260 Bandley Drive, Cupertino, CA 95014.
Architecture	Desktop with 6502 microprocessor.
Maximum RAM Memory Capacity	48K bytes.
Mass Storage Device With Base Unit	Cassette interface provided, recorder not provided, 1600 bits per second.
Price with Base RAM	$1195 (16K) suggested retail.

APPLE II AND APPLE II PLUS
(Continued)

Price with Maximum RAM

$1495 (48K).

Display Type

Color or black and white television with rf modulator (not supplied by Apple) or color or black and white monitor.

Screen Format

Text: 40 columns by 24 lines, uppercase only, 2 pages provided. Graphics: low resolution—40 horizontal by 48 vertical elements, high resolution—280 horizontal by 192 vertical elements (53,760 dots). Four line text scrolling window in graphics modes.

Number of Colors

High resolution—6, low resolution—15.

Sound Capability

Built-in 3-inch speaker, machine language tone driver program in the programmers aid ROM.

Expandability

Eight built-in 50-pin peripheral board connectors. They are fully buffered with interrupt and DMA priority structure provided to 6502 microprocessor.

Software Media

Cassette, disk, and plug in ROMs (not ROM packs).

Special Features

Game I/O connector with 4 paddle inputs, 3 TTL inputs, 4 TTL outputs. Shape graphics statements from BASIC-rotate and scale objects.

APPLE II AND APPLE II PLUS
(Continued)

Comments   First color graphics computer for home and hobby, today has huge base of exciting color software, especially excellent animation games. Super for engineer types. Great graphics programmability. Largest number of peripherals available for a desktop unit (due to 8 connector slots). The Apple II Plus has Applesoft (floating point) BASIC instead of Integer BASIC, and some minor start-up differences.

APPLE III PROFESSIONAL SYSTEM

Name and Model Number
Apple III™ Professional Computer System.

Manufacturer's Name and Address
Apple Computer Inc., 10260 Bandley Drive, Cupertino, CA 95014.

Architecture
Desktop with 6502A microprocessor.

Maximum RAM Memory Capacity
128K bytes.

Mass Storage Device With Base Unit
Built-in 5-inch floppy disk drive with 140K bytes per diskette, up to 3 additional drives may be daisy chained. No cassette interface.

Price with Base RAM
$3490 (96K) suggested retail.

APPLE III PROFESSIONAL SYSTEM
(Continued)

Price with Maximum RAM
$3990 (128K) suggested retail.

Display Type
Requires additional color or black and white monitor, color unit from Apple is available. Has NTSC and RGB outputs.

Screen Format
Text: 80 columns by 24 lines, black and white, 40 by 24, 16 color, or 40 by 24, upper- and lower-case, normal or inverse black and white video. Graphics: 280 horizontal elements by 192 vertical elements in 16 colors up to 560 by 192 in black and white (107,520 dots). Software selectable character set. Plus all Apple II modes.

Number of Colors
16 in medium resolution, none in highest resolution.

Sound Capability
Built-in 2-inch speaker, output of 6-bit D to A converter or by fixed frequency beep generator.

Expandability
Four 50-pin expansion slots inside cabinet (not Apple II compatible). RS-232-C DB-25 connector and serial I/O built-in. Two DB-9's for up to four joysticks and Apple printer.

Software Media
Mini-diskettes.

Special Features
Emulation mode turns the Apple III into an Apple II and runs most Apple II software. Self-diagnostic prints out any errors in its hardware. Built-in real time clock.

APPLE III PROFESSIONAL SYSTEM
(Continued)

Comments   Apple's new computer system is a step in the direction of small business and professional plus color and sound capability.

ATARI 400

Name and Model Number	Atari 400.
Manufacturer's Name and Address	Atari, Inc., 1265 Borregas Ave., Sunnyvale, CA 94086.
Architecture	Desktop with 6502 microprocessor and 4 custom Atari chips. Touch sensitive keyboard.
Maximum RAM Memory Capacity	16K bytes (Atari 800 is 48K).

ATARI 400
(Continued)

Mass Storage Device With Base Unit	Cassette interface and recorder included, motor controllable from BASIC.
Price with Base RAM	$499.95 (8K).
Price with Maximum RAM	$630.00 (16K).
Display Type	Color or black and white television. FCC approved rf modulator built-in.
Screen Format	Text: 40 columns by 24 lines, upper-case and lower-case, 3 additional text modes for larger characters. Graphics: 40h by 20v elements to 320h by 192v elements. Up to 57 built-in graphics characters.
Number of Colors	Two colors in 320h by 192v mode. Up to 16 colors in lowest resolution. Up to 16 levels of luminance (brightness).
Sound Capability	Four channel sound chip outputs to television sound circuits. Each channel has independent frequency, noise, and volume control.
Expandability	Same as 800 except maximum RAM is only 16K so certain graphics modes are not available.
Software Media	Cassette, disk and plug-in ROM cartridges. Room for two program cartridges is provided in the Atari flip up top.

ATARI 400
(Continued)

Special Features FCC approved modulator, automatic motor control on cassette recorder, four controller ports, four internal cartridge slots for memory, good Atari software.

Comments The Atari 400 is made for those not wishing to spend as much as the 800 costs, but still have many of the major features. The 400 has a touch sensitive keyboard instead of the regular depression type keyboard. It comes with 8K RAM expandable to 16K.

ATARI 800

Name and Model Number   Atari 800.

Manufacturer's Name and Address   Atari, Inc., 1265 Borregas Ave., Sunnyvale, CA 94086.

Architecture   Desktop with 6502 microprocessor.

ATARI 800
(Continued)

Maximum RAM Memory Capacity	48K bytes.
Mass Storage Device With Base Unit	Cassette interface and recorder included, motor controllable from BASIC.
Price with Base RAM	$1080 (8K).
Price with Maximum RAM	$1480 (48K).
Display Type	Color or black and white television. FCC approved rf modulator built-in.
Screen Format	Text: 40 columns by 24 lines, uppercase and lower-case, 3 additional text modes for larger characters. Graphics: 40h by 20v elements to 320h by 192v elements. Up to 57 built-in graphics characters.
Number of Colors	Two colors in 320h by 192v mode. Up to 16 colors in lowest resolution. Up to 16 levels of luminance (brightness).
Sound Capability	Four channel sound chip outputs to television sound circuits. Each channel has independent frequency, noise, and volume control.
Expandability	Uses serial bus system to reduce interference. Requires a 4 slot interface module to add additional peripherals. Game paddles and cassette plug into connectors in front of unit.

ATARI 800
(Continued)

Software Media   Cassette, disk and plug-in ROM cartridges. Room for two program car-
tridges is provided in the Atari flip-up
top.

Special Features   FCC approved modulator, automatic
motor control on cassette recorder,
four controller ports, four internal cartridge slots for memory, good Atari
software.

Comments   An incredible product with superior
sound synthesis and graphics anima-
tion capability. Four custom chips
built into this machine that give it
DMA object animation for very realis-
tic control of objects, automatic col-
lision detection, etc.

COMMODORE PET 4000 SERIES

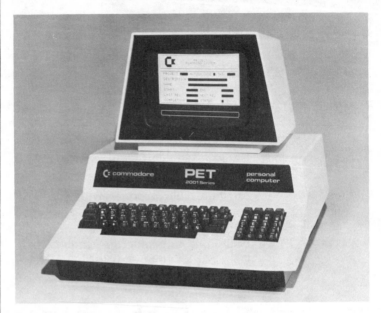

Name and Model Number	PET 4000 Series.
Manufacturer's Name and Address	Commodore Business Machines, Inc., 950 Rittenhouse Road, Norristown, PA 19403.
Architecture	Desktop with crt uses 6502 microprocessor.
Maximum RAM Memory Capacity	32K bytes.
Mass Storage Device With Base Unit	Two cassette interface ports included, recorder optional.

COMMODORE PET 4000 SERIES
(Continued)

Price with Base RAM $795 (8K).

Price with Maximum RAM $1295 (32K).

Display Type   Built-in 9-inch crt with green phosphor for low eye fatigue.

Screen Format   Text: 40 columns by 25 lines, uppercase only on 8 by 8 matrix, normal, inverse, or flashing characters. Graphics: 64 graphics characters (famous PET set) in 8 by 8 matrix. Equivalent to indirect graphics resolution of 320h by 200v.

Number of Colors   None.

Sound Capability   None, but port can be used for speaker.

Expandability   4 integral plug connectors for I/O, IEEE 488 instrument bus provided can have up to 10 daisy-chained devices. No game controls.

Software Media   Cassette tape, mini-disks.

Special Features   73-key keyboard with graphics characters etched on face of each key, green screen is easy to look at for extended periods, 9 digit BASIC.

COMMODORE PET 4000 SERIES
(Continued)

Comments

The famous PET computer is very popular among schools and especially in Europe. Graphics are somewhat difficult to apply and dots are not directly accessible, but a huge base of software exists for the PET. This was the first integrated computer (crt+keyboard+computer). The first PETs had a calculator-like keyboard which caused controversy, and a built-in cassette recorder (see insert). These are still marketed in Europe.

COMMODORE CBM 8000 SERIES

Name and Model Number CBM 8000 Series.

Manufacturer's Name and Address Commodore Business Machines, Inc., 950 Rittenhouse Road, Norristown, PA 19403.

Architecture Desktop with crt uses 6502 microprocessor.

Maximum RAM Memory Capacity 32K bytes.

Mass Storage Device With Base Unit Two cassette interface ports included, recorder optional.

COMMODORE CBM 8000 SERIES
(Continued)

Price with Base RAM $1295 (16K).

Price with Maximum RAM $1795 (32K).

Display Type   Built-in 9-inch crt with green phosphor for low eye fatigue.

Screen Format   Text: 80 columns by 25 lines, 128 upper-case and lower-case characters on 8 by 8 matrix, normal, inverse, or flashing characters. Graphics: 128 graphics characters (famous PET set plus more) in 8 by 8 matrix.

Number of Colors   None.

Sound Capability   None, but port can be used for speaker.

Expandability   4 integral plug connectors for I/O, IEEE 488 instrument bus provided can have up to 10 daisy-chained devices. No game controls.

Software Media   Cassette tape, mini-disks.

Special Features   73-key keyboard with graphics ability, numeric keypad, green screen is easy to look at for extended periods, 9 digit BASIC.

COMMODORE CBM 8000 SERIES
(Continued)

Comments

This is Commodore's grown up PET computer designed for small business users. Has higher resolution 80 by 25 screen. Lots of peripherals available. Good selection of software including word processing and client accounting.

CROMEMCO SYSTEM THREE

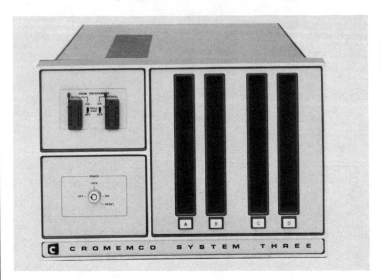

Name and Model Number	Cromemco System Three.
Manufacturer's Name and Address	Cromemco, Inc., 280 Bernadrdo Ave., Mountain View, CA 94040.
Architecture	Mainframe with 21 slot S-100 bus using Z-80A microprocessor.
Maximum RAM Memory Capacity	512K bytes (using bank selection and multiple 64K RAM boards).
Mass Storage Device With Base Unit	Two built-in 8-inch double density double sided floppy disk drives.
Price with Base RAM	$7395 (64K).

CROMEMCO SYSTEM THREE
(Continued)

Price with Maximum RAM

$16,220 (320K).

Display Type

Requires standard serial terminal with 80h by 24v screen (about $700-$1000 new) or video board and external video monitor.

Screen Format

Not applicable, depends on terminal or video board used.

Number of Colors

Not applicable unless Cromemco 16 color board is used in which case resolution is 756h by 484v pixels (cost $1785) and requires a color RGB monitor (about $3000).

Sound Capability

None with base unit but Cromemco JS-1 joystick console with speaker available for $95.00.

Expandability

21 slots give great expansion capability. Can use any of S-100 boards on the market, as long as they say they will run on the Cromemco S-100 bus (see S-100 bus).

Software Media

Double density 8-inch diskettes.

Special Features

RS-232-C interface, 30-amp power supply, rack or bench mounted, locking front panel.

CROMEMCO SYSTEM THREE
(Continued)

Comments   Cromemco is, in the microcomputer field, a most mature company, and its product line has been perfected over the years while other S-100 manufacturers failed. The company is known for its conservative approach to design and has a large assortment of professional software.

CROMEMCO Z-2H

Name and Model Number

Cromemco Z-2H.

Manufacturer's Name and Address

Cromemco, Inc., 280 Bernadrdo Ave., Mountain View, CA 94040.

Architecture

Same mainframe with 21 slot S-100 bus using Z-80A microprocessor as System Three, except contains a built-in 11 megabyte hard disk drive and controller, plus two quad density mini disks for backup, and a 12 slot motherboard with 5 slots occupied with Cromemco boards.

Maximum RAM Memory Capacity

512K bytes (using bank selection and multiple 64K RAM boards).

CROMEMCO Z-2H
(Continued)

Mass Storage Device With Base Unit	11 megabyte hard disk with 5.6 megabit per second transfer rate and two quad density disk drives (about 780K bytes combined).
Price with Base RAM	$9995 (64K).
Price with Maximum RAM	$19,810 (320K).
Display Type	Requires standard serial terminal with 80h by 24v screen (about $700-$1000 new) or video board and external video monitor.
Screen Format	Not applicable, depends on terminal or video board used.
Number of Colors	Not applicable unless Cromemco 16 color board is used in which case resolution is 756h by 484v pixels (cost $1785) and requires a color RGB monitor (about $3000).
Sound Capability	None with base unit but Cromemco JS-1 joystick console with speaker available for $95.00.
Expandability	21 slots give great expansion capability. Can use any of S-100 boards on the market, as long as they say they will run on the Cromemco S-100 bus (see S-100 bus).
Software Media	Double density 8-inch diskettes.

CROMEMCO Z-2H
(Continued)

Special Features   RS-232-C interface, 30-amp power supply, rack or bench mounted, locking front panel.

Comments   The Z-2H (H for hard disk) is available without the hard disk, with or without RAM, disk drives, and so on, from $995. The hard disk alone is $7000. Normally the Z-2H is used in rack mounted configuration (19 inch). Has built-in 4K ROM firmware monitor, power on jump circuitry, diagnostics, etc.

CROMEMCO SYSTEM ZERO

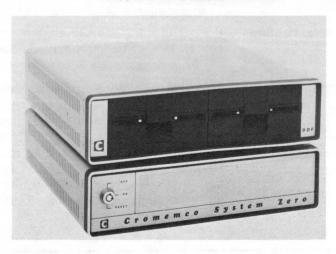

Name and Model Number	Cromemco System Zero.
Manufacturer's Name and Address	Cromemco, Inc., 280 Bernadrdo Ave., Mountain View, CA 94040.
Architecture	Small S-100 mainframe with 4 slots.
Maximum RAM Memory Capacity	64K bytes.
Mass Storage Device With Base Unit	Not equipped but matching quad density mini disk drives available for $1295.
Price with Base RAM	$995 (1K).

CROMEMCO SYSTEM ZERO
(Continued)

Price with Maximum RAM

$2780 (64K) $2995 with disk controller built in.

Display Type

Requires standard serial terminal with 80h by 24v screen (about $700-$1000 new) or video board and external video monitor.

Screen Format

Not applicable, depends on terminal or video board used.

Number of Colors

Not applicable unless Cromemco 16 color board is used in which case resolution is 756h by 484v pixels (cost $1785) and requires a color RGB monitor (about $3000).

Sound Capability

None with base unit but Cromemco JS-1 joystick console with speaker available for $95.00.

Expandability

21 slots give great expansion capability. Can use any of S-100 boards on the market, as long as they say they will run on the Cromemco S-100 bus (see S-100 bus).

Software Media

Double density 8-inch diskettes.

Special Features

RS-232-C interface, 30 amp power supply, rack or bench mounted, locking front panel.

Comments

The System Zero rounds out Cromemco's product line. The Zero is a low board capacity unit with a Z-80 microprocessor, 64K byte RAM board, and disk controller, which leaves only one more slot for S-100 expansion.

DYNABYTE 8/2

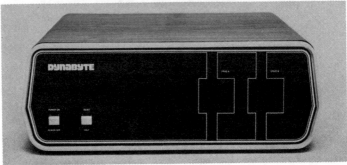

Name and Model Number   Dynabyte 8/2 Dual 5 inch Disk Microcomputer.

Manufacturer's Name and Address   Dynabyte, 115 Independence Drive, Menlo Park, CA 94025.

Architecture   S-100 mainframe.

Maximum RAM Memory Capacity   64K bytes.

DYNABYTE 8/2
(Continued)

Mass Storage Device With Base Unit	Built-in dual 5-inch floppy disk drives.
Price with Base RAM	$4895 (48K).
Price with Maximum RAM	$5295 (64K).
Display Type	External serial terminal required, two serial ports provided.
Screen Format	Not applicable.
Number of Colors	Not applicable.
Sound Capability	None.
Expandability	12 S-100 bus connectors provided in heavy duty shielded metal mainframe.
Software Media	Double density mini-floppy diskettes.
Special Features	10 interval timers, 8 levels of interrupt, 100 to 76,800 baud, real time clock, preregulated power supply, modular design, light on/off, real woodgrain finish.
Comments	A very nice S-100 computer which is very popular in small business uses.

EXIDY SORCERER

Name and Model Number	Exidy Sorcerer.
Manufacturer's Name and Address	Exidy, Inc., Data Products Division, 969 West Maude Ave., Sunnyvale, CA 94086.
Architecture	Desktop using Z-80 microprocessor.
Maximum RAM Memory Capacity	32K bytes.
Mass Storage Device With Base Unit	ROM PAC™ cartridges, dual cassette I/O ports are provided, recorders not included.
Price with Base RAM	$895 list (8K), $1150 (16K).

EXIDY SORCERER
(Continued)

Price with Maximum RAM

$1395 list (32K).

Display Type

Requires separate crt monitor. Exidy provides 12-inch unit with high resolution P31 phosphor for $299.

Screen Format

Text: 64 columns by 30 lines, 128 ASCII characters include upper-case and lower-case (duplicates the popular PET set of characters). Graphics: 64 horizontal elements by 30 vertical elements, in an 8 by 8 matrix. 64 fixed graphics characters (PET set) and 64 user definable characters. Indirect 540h by 240v resolution.

Number of Colors

None.

Sound Capability

None.

Expandability

S-100 bus expansion connector. Requires Exidy Expansion Unit which is a 6 slot S-100 chassis style like the Sorcerer ($299).

Software Media

ROM PAKs (program cartridges), cassette tapes.

Special Features

The Sorcerer's trump card is that it has S-100 bus expansion capability. Requires an expansion box with motherboard, slots, etc., to hold the S-100 boards. 300 or 1200 baud RS-232-C interface. PET set of characters.

EXIDY SORCERER
(Continued)

Comments

Exidy was the first company to provide several personal computer innovations. They were the first with plug-in ROM software as well as the first personal computer with an S-100 interface expansion. The Exidy has a very high graphics resolution, but, like the PET, it is not directly accessible.

HEATHKIT H-8

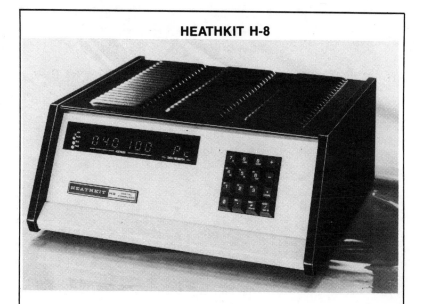

Name and Model Number	Heathkit H-8.
Manufacturer's Name and Address	Heath Company, Benton Harbor, MI 49022.
Architecture	Mainframe in kit form with 8080A.
Maximum RAM Memory Capacity	64K bytes.
Mass Storage Device With Base Unit	None, requires separate serial cassette interface board to use with cassette ($99.00).
Price with Base RAM	$394 kit (4K RAM board), $598 kit (16K).

HEATHKIT H-8
(Continued)

Price with Maximum RAM
$1869 (four 16K boards).

Display Type
Built-in 9-digit octal LED display is part of machine's intelligent hardware front panel. Requires separate terminal and I/O interface board to use full power.

Screen Format
Nine digits, in octal, 4 LEDs.

Number of Colors
Not applicable.

Sound Capability
Built-in speaker reacts to keyboard entry.

Expandability
Heath's own 50-pin bus with seven slots provided.

Software Media
Cassette and floppy disk.

Special Features
Kit form, intelligent front panel display and keypad allows debugging and hardware operations without crt or terminal. Ideal for experimenters and educators.

Comments
The only mainframe kit on the market, the H-8 was Heath's first entry in the computer market. Memory is a bit expensive, but there are several companies offering cheaper memory. Quality is extremely high. Manuals are models for the industry.

HEATHKIT H-11A

Name and Model Number	Heathkit H-11A.
Manufacturer's Name and Address	Heath Company, Benton Harbor, MI 49022.
Architecture	Mainframe in kit form with DEC® LSI-11 compatibility. Uses 16-bit PDP-11 equivalent KD-11-HA CPU set.
Maximum RAM Memory Capacity	32K words (16-bit word).
Mass Storage Device With Base Unit	None, requires separate floppy disk drive interface board and drives ($1995 kit).
Price with Base RAM	$1290 kit (4K RAM board), $1675 (16K).

HEATHKIT H-11A
(Continued)

Price with Maximum RAM
$2155 kit (two 16K boards).

Display Type
Requires external serial terminal, such as Heath H-19 kit ($675 kit).

Screen Format
Not applicable.

Number of Colors
Not applicable.

Sound Capability
None.

Expandability
Eight Heathkit designated bus connectors inside mainframe.

Software Media
8-inch floppy diskette.

Special Features
Kit form, switching power supply, ROM based console routines, 380 ns 16-bit processor, executes PDP-11/34 instruction set.

Comments
The only other mainframe kit on the market, the H-11 is a Digital Equipment Corporation LSI-11 converted by Heath's skilled engineers into a beautiful kit. It is capable of running the gigantic amount of software that exists for the PDP-11. However this software is generally applicable to large businesses who can afford the PDP-11/34, so this may not be a big advantage if you are a small user. Quality is extremely high. Again manuals are models for the industry.

HEATHKIT H-89 ALL-IN-ONE

Name and Model Number	Heathkit H-89 All-In-One.
Manufacturer's Name and Address	Heath Company, Benton Harbor, MI 49022.
Architecture	Desktop in kit form with built-in crt monitor. Uses two Z-80 microprocessors.
Maximum RAM Memory Capacity	48K bytes.
Mass Storage Device With Base Unit	Built-in single density mini-floppy disk drive and cassette tape interface.
Price with Base RAM	$1695 kit (16K).

HEATHKIT H-89 ALL-IN-ONE
(Continued)

Price with Maximum RAM $2895 (48K) assembled price.

Display Type Built-in 12-inch high resolution black and white crt.

Screen Format Text: 80 columns by 24 lines, 5 by 7 dot matrix upper-case, 5 by 9 for lower-case with descenders. Special 25th line nonscrolling status line. Graphics: 33 built-in graphics characters on an 8 by 10 dot matrix accessible via BASIC PRINT and CHR$ commands.

Number of Colors Not applicable.

Sound Capability None.

Expandability Two serial ports, no bus output or expansion, but disk expansion coming.

Software Media Mini-disk, cassette.

Special Features High quality crt with P4 phosphor, numeric keypad, two Z-80s allow terminal and computer to run independently. Extra 16K of RAM is $150.

Comments A very nicely designed computer and second to the PET to go totally integrated (crt+keyboard+disk in one box). Build it yourself to discover the workings of a computer. Heath now provides CP/M on all their products which makes it a good deal.

HEWLETT-PACKARD HP-85

Name and Model Number

Hewlett Packard HP-85.

Manufacturer's Name and Address

Hewlett Packard, 1000 N.E. Circle Blvd., Corvallis, OR 97330.

Architecture

Desktop with built-in crt and printer.

Maximum RAM Memory Capacity

32K bytes.

Mass Storage Device With Base Unit

16K bytes.

Price with Base RAM

$3250 (16K).

Price with Maximum RAM

$3645 (32K).

HEWLETT-PACKARD HP-85
(Continued)

Display Type   Built-in high resolution 5-inch diagonal display, adjustable intensity.

Screen Format   Text: 32 columns by 16 lines, 5 by 7 dot matrix characters, upper-case only. Graphics: 256 horizontal elements by 192 vertical elements with BASIC graphic commands.

Number of Colors   None.

Sound Capability   Built-in speaker and machine language beep driver. Controllable tone and duration.

Expandability   Four different I/O ports: HP-IB, RS-232-C, GP-IO, BCD.

Software Media   Magnetic Tape Cartridge (195K bytes program capacity, 210K bytes data capacity, rewind in 29 seconds, 42 max files per tape), and ROM interface and language modules.

Special Features   Built-in silent thermal printer, incredibly well designed 65 statement BASIC, 12 digit accuracy, exponent of 10 to the 499 power, ROM drawer holds 6 ROMs.

HEWLETT-PACKARD HP-85
(Continued)

Comments

In the tradition of the world's finest electronic instrument maker, the Hewlett Packard HP-85 is in a class by itself. Like all HP equipment, the price is higher than usual, but the completeness and packaging of the HP-85 is uncomparable. The printer can produce anything on the graphics screen, rotated 90°. The ROM drawer holds modules that perform instrument interfacing for various I/O ports. Perfect to serve as an instrument controller.

ISC COMPUCOLOR II

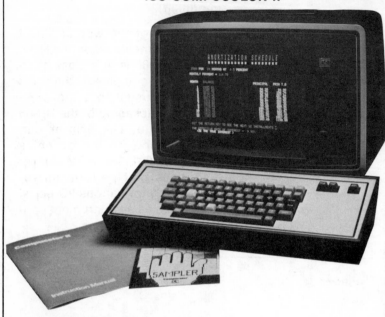

Name and Model Number	Compucolor II.
Manufacturer's Name and Address	Compucolor Corporation, PO Box 569, Norcross, GA 30071.
Architecture	Desktop with 8080A microprocessor.
Maximum RAM Memory Capacity	32K bytes.
Mass Storage Device With Base Unit	5¼-inch mini-disk drive.

ISC COMPUCOLOR II
(Continued)

Price with Base RAM
$1495 (8K).

Price with Maximum RAM
$1995 (32K).

Display Type
Built-in 11-inch color monitor.

Screen Format
Text: 64 columns by 32 lines with two different character sizes. 64 upper-case only with additional 64 graphics characters. Graphics: 128 horizontal elements by 128 vertical elements, plotting and vector commands from BASIC.

Number of Colors
Eight colors.

Sound Capability
None.

Expandability
50 pin bus requires expansion box to plug additional peripherals into computer. Has RS-232-C asynchronous channel for printer or modem.

Software Media
5¼-inch mini-diskettes.

Special Features
Very powerful crt terminal commands (sends escape codes in PRINT or CHR$ commands), 15 plot modes, nice DOS, 30 I/O ports.

Comments
Little brother (or sister) to Intercolor machines from ISC (see Intercolor).

ISC INTERCOLOR 8000 SERIES

Name and Model Number	Intercolor 8001 (shown).
Manufacturer's Name and Address	Intelligent Systems Corp., 225 Technology Park/Atlanta, Norcross, GA 30092.
Architecture	Desktop with built-in color crt. Many options available for screen size, cabinet, etc. Uses 8080 microprocessor.
Maximum RAM Memory Capacity	48K bytes.
Mass Storage Device With Base Unit	Cassette interface option, floppy disk interface option.

ISC INTERCOLOR 8000 SERIES
(Continued)

Price with Base RAM $1895 (16K).

Price with Maximum RAM $3040 (48K).

Display Type   13-inch or 19-inch built-in color crt.

Screen Format   Text: 80 columns by 40 lines (highest of any unit), upper-case only, 2 character heights. Graphics: 160h by 192v elements (option G $2395), 384h by 480v elements (option H $3795).

Number of Colors   Eight foreground, eight background.

Sound Capability   None.

Expandability   No bus, RS-232-C serial port for printer or modem, plus disk I/O connector.

Software Media   Cassette, floppy disk, hard disk.

Special Features   Powerful editing modes, CP/M version, color coordinated keycaps, pure colors due to color monitor, business BASIC.

Comments   A truly special computer for those interested in color graphics.

MATTEL INTELLIVISION

Name and Model Number

Mattel Intellivision.

Manufacturer's Name and Address

Mattel Electronics, a division of Mattel Inc., 5150 Rosecrans Avenue, Hawthorne, CA 90250.

Architecture

Desktop color unit with GI 1610 16-bit microprocessor in master component and 6502 microprocessor for optional keyboard element.

Maximum RAM Memory Capacity

64K bytes.

Mass Storage Device With Base Unit

Built-in cassette recorder in optional keyboard component.

MATTEL INTELLIVISION
(Continued)

Price with Base RAM	$300 (2K).
Price with Maximum RAM	$800 (18K).
Display Type	Requires color or black and white television, rf modulator is built in.
Screen Format	Text: 20 columns by 12 lines, uppercase and lower-case in an 8×8 matrix. With keyboard component 40 columns by 24 lines. Graphics: 160 horizontal elements by 192 vertical elements, with 8 moving foreground symbols from 64 graphics characters.
Number of Colors	16.
Sound Capability	Crash and cheering sounds generator chip in master component, audio tracks on cassettes in keyboard element.
Expandability	Two 44-pin I/O connectors in keyboard element. Microphone jack. Master component alone is not programmable.
Software Media	Cassette tapes and ROM program cartridges.
Special Features	Two universal hand controllers, 16 direction overlay pads, nice graphics.

MATTEL INTELLIVISION
(Continued)

Comments

The Mattel unit is a video game that can grow up and be a more powerful computer. You purchase the keyboard component and drop the master component into it. The Mattel people have gone all the way on software and have used popular personalities to create their software: Jack LaLanne for an exercise program, a football game officialized by NFL, etc.

NORTHSTAR HORIZON

Name and Model Number
NorthStar Horizon.

Manufacturer's Name and Address
NorthStar Computers, Inc., 1440 Fourth Street, Berkeley, CA 94710.

Architecture
S-100 mainframe, available kit or assembled. Uses Z-80 microprocessor.

Maximum RAM Memory Capacity
64K bytes.

Mass Storage Device With Base Unit
Two built-in mini-floppy diskettes, double or quad density.

Price with Base RAM
$1789 (16K double density kit).

Price with Maximum RAM
$3830 (64K DD, assembled).

NORTHSTAR HORIZON
(Continued)

Display Type   Separate serial terminal or video board and monitor required.

Screen Format   Not applicable.

Number of Colors Not applicable.

Sound Capability None.

Expandability   12 slot S-100 motherboard.

Software Media   Mini-diskettes.

Special Features Kit or assembled, good prices, runs CP/M, serial I/O búilt-in to motherboard, along with disk power supply regulation and real-time clock.

Comments   Prices are up to $500 less if ordered through mail. NorthStar provides their own DOS and BASIC. Nice wood finish and well constructed metal frame, two serial and one parallel I/O port for printer, terminal, etc. Good manuals. Hard disk available.

OHIO SCIENTIFIC SUPERBOARD

Name and Model Number	Ohio Scientific Superboard.
Manufacturer's Name and Address	Ohio Scientific, 1333 South Chillicothe Road, Aurora, OH 44202.
Architecture	Desktop available as just single board, with or without cabinet, power supply, etc. Makes up the Challenger series. Uses 6502 microprocessor.
Maximum RAM Memory Capacity	8K bytes on board, 32K with extension board.
Mass Storage Device With Base Unit	Built-in Kansas City cassette interface, recorder not supplied.

OHIO SCIENTIFIC SUPERBOARD
(Continued)

Price with Base RAM — $279 (4K).

Price with Maximum RAM — $577 (8K, using extension board).

Display Type — External black and white monitor or television required. Modulator not supplied.

Screen Format — Text: 24 columns by 24 rows, monitor allows up to 30 by 30.

Number of Colors — None, but separate color board available.

Sound Capability — None, but separate sound board available.

Expandability — Requires separate expander board (610) which contains room for 32K of RAM in 4K increments ($79.00 each), and has circuitry for two mini floppy disk drives. Many I/O boards with interfaces to joysticks, ac remote control, etc.

Software Media — Cassette tape or mini-floppy diskette.

Special Features — Single board computer allows a wide range of configurations to be purchased. You can buy just the bare board, the cabinet and other parts later, or use your own, and so on. Home controller interfaces available for computer based phone answering machine, home security system, etc.

OHIO SCIENTIFIC SUPERBOARD
(Continued)

Comments A good price for a starting system.
Screen format is low resolution but
color board extends this.

RADIO SHACK TRS-80 COLOR COMPUTER

Name and Model Number	TRS-80 Color Computer.
Manufacturer's Name and Address	Radio Shack, a division of Tandy Corporation, 1300 One Tandy Center, Fort Worth, TX 76102.
Architecture	Desktop color unit with MP6809E microprocessor.
Maximum RAM Memory Capacity	16K bytes.
Mass Storage Device With Base Unit	Cassette interface (1500BPS) included, recorder not included.

RADIO SHACK TRS-80 COLOR COMPUTER
(Continued)

Price with Base RAM	$399 (4K).
Price with Maximum RAM	$518 (16K).
Display Type	Color or black and white television or monitor, rf modulator built in, Radio Shack provides a 13-inch color television with tuner for $399.
Screen Format	Text: 32 columns by 16 lines, all upper-case. Graphics: 64 horizontal by 32 vertical elements to 256h by 196v in five graphics modes. High resolution modes require larger memory.
Number of Colors	8 colors in lowest resolution, 2 colors in highest resolution.
Sound Capability	No speaker but port provided for one.
Expandability	No real bus, but typical RS-232-C serial port, joystick connector, disk drive expansion connector.
Software Media	Cassette, ROM Program Cartridges, Diskettes.
Special Features	Extended 16K color BASIC has rotation and zoom, has machine language capability, first non-Z-80 computer from Radio Shack.

RADIO SHACK TRS-80 COLOR COMPUTER
(Continued)

Comments

Tandy's first entry into the color desktop color computer market. Not as powerful as the Atari in its graphics, but the price ($518 with 16K) is quite good for a computer of this caliber. The 6809 microprocessor is internally a 16-bit device and very powerful (See *Microcomputer Primer,* second edition, Howard W. Sams & Co., Inc., catalog number 21653, page 166, for details on this processor.) Optional Extended BASIC offers 9-digit accuracy, real-time clock, user definable keys, etc.

RADIO SHACK TRS-80 POCKET COMPUTER

Name and Model Number	TRS-80 Pocket Computer.
Manufacturer's Name and Address	Radio Shack, a division of Tandy Corporation, 1300 One Tandy Center, Fort Worth, TX 76102.
Architecture	Handheld unit with dual 4-bit CMOS microprocessors, 300 hour battery back up on memory.
Maximum RAM Memory Capacity	1.9K bytes.
Mass Storage Device With Base Unit	Cassette interface (1500BPS) included, optional recorder not included, available for $49.00.
Price with Base RAM	$249.95 (1.9K).

RADIO SHACK TRS-80 POCKET COMPUTER
(Continued)

Price with Maximum RAM   Same.

Display Type   Revolutionary 24-character Liquid Crystal Display (LCD).

Screen Format   Text: 24 horizontal characters displayable at one time, on a 5 by 7 dot matrix, up to 80 may be stored in buffer and scrolled out under computer control.

Number of Colors   None.

Sound Capability   Built-in buzzer accessible from BASIC with BEEP command.

Expandability   None other than cassette interface.

Software Media   Cassette tapes.

Special Features   300-hour battery, CMOS memory retains data when unit is turned off, auto-turn-off after 7 minutes without use, 57 QWERTY keypad, 18 keys are reserved for BASIC commands for easy entry of programs.

RADIO SHACK TRS-80 POCKET COMPUTER
(Continued)

Comments
Tandy's first entry into the handheld computer market (still pretty much virgin territory in United States, some activity in Japan) is a well designed unit. Has a great deal of features for such a low price ($249). It is still to be shown that the handheld is a major market, and the Tandy's lack of expandability may hold it back. Level-I like BASIC has 15 arithmetic functions, 7 character string variables, 26 data element memory, and 48 step reversible memory for storing functions, even when power is off.

RADIO SHACK TRS-80 MODEL III

Name and Model Number	TRS-80 Model III.
Manufacturer's Name and Address	Radio Shack, a division of Tandy Corporation, 1300 One Tandy Center, Fort Worth, TX 76102.
Architecture	Desktop unit with space for two mini-disk drives. Uses 2 MHz Z-80 microprocessor.
Maximum RAM Memory Capacity	48K bytes.
Mass Storage Device With Base Unit	Two speed cassette inteface: 500BPS for Model I compatibility and 1500-BPS high speed.

RADIO SHACK TRS-80 MODEL III
(Continued)

Price with Base RAM

$699 (4K Level I system).

Price with Maximum RAM

$999 for 16K w/Model III BASIC, $2495 for 32K w/dual 5-inch mini-disk drives, additional 16K RAM $299.

Display Type

Built-in 12-inch high resolution monitor.

Screen Format

Same as TRS-80 Model I. Text: 64 columns by 16 lines (also 32 by 16 format), upper-case only in 8 by 8 matrix. Graphics: 128 horizontal elements by 48 vertical elements. 2 by 3 matrix cell may be used in PRINT statements.

Number of Colors

None.

Sound Capability

None.

Expandability

Same 40 pin bus connector as on Model I, uses external Expansion Interface Unit box to implement additional bus connectors.

Software Media

Cassettes, diskettes.

Special Features

65-key keyboard, 12-key datapad, real-time clock accessible from Model III BASIC, RS-232-C board may be installed to inside of computer.

RADIO SHACK TRS-80 MODEL III
(Continued)

Comments   The Model III is Tandy's bridge between the early Model I and the more powerful Model II. It is compatible with all Model I software and can read its tapes, and can read a higher speed 1500 baud tape as well. For some the screen is not wide enough, but some company will probably offer an adaptor to make it an 80 character by 24 line. The $699 price and its ability to grow up to a larger more powerful unit should make the Model III a hit on the market.

RADIO SHACK TRS-80 MODEL II

Name and Model Number	TRS-80 Model II.
Manufacturer's Name and Address	Radio Shack, a divison of Tandy Corporation, 1300 One Tandy Center, Fort Worth, TX 76102.
Architecture	Desktop unit (aimed at small business user) with built-in 8-inch floppy disk drive. Uses Z-80 microprocessor.
Maximum RAM Memory Capacity	64K bytes.
Mass Storage Device With Base Unit	Built-in 8-inch floppy disk drive.
Price with Base RAM	$3450 (32K bytes).

RADIO SHACK TRS-80 MODEL II
(Continued)

Price with Maximum RAM

$3899 (64K bytes).

Display Type

12-inch built-in crt, upper-case and lower-case with descenders.

Screen Format

80 columns by 24 lines.

Number of Colors

None.

Sound Capability

None.

Expandability

Same 40-pin bus connector as on Model I, uses external Expansion Interface Unit box to implement additional bus connectors.

Software Media

Cassettes, 8-inch diskettes.

Special Features

Numeric keypad, large screen, on-site service, business orientation, 8-inch double density drive stores ½ million bytes.

Comments

The Model II TRS-80 is Radio Shack's business computer. It has a large complement of business software (General Ledger, Payroll, Word Processing, etc.) available in the $200-$400 price range and a fairly wide selection of peripherals—printers, desk stands, extra disk drives, etc. An additional 8-inch disk drive is $1150. Competes with numerous S-100 business computers.

RADIO SHACK TRS-80 MODEL I

Name and Model Number	TRS-80 Model I.
Manufacturer's Name and Address	Radio Shack, a division of Tandy Corporation, 1300 One Tandy Center, Fort Worth, TX 76102.
Architecture	Desktop unit with cables interconnecting keyboard, expansion box and monitor. Uses Z-80 microprocessor.
Maximum RAM Memory Capacity	48K bytes.
Mass Storage Device With Base Unit	500BPS cassette interface.
Price with Base RAM	$499 (4K Level I system).

RADIO SHACK TRS-80 MODEL I
(Continued)

Price with Maximum RAM $1446 (48K Level II system).

Display Type   Detached black and white monitor provided.

Screen Format   Text: 64 columns by 16 lines (also 32 by 16 format), upper-case only in 8 by 8 matrix. Graphics: 128 horizontal elements by 48 vertical elements. 2 by 3 matrix cell may be used in PRINT statements.

Number of Colors   None.

Sound Capability   None.

Expandability   40 pin "male" bus connector is accessible through tacky little door on rear of keyboard. Requires external Expansion Interface Unit box to implement additional bus connectors ($299).

Software Media   Cassettes, diskettes.

Special Features   Two types of BASIC (Level I and Level II) available.

RADIO SHACK TRS-80 MODEL I
(Continued)

Comments

The Model I was for Tandy like the Model T was for Ford, it was rough in spots but it got the job done. The Model I was Tandy's first computer product and it caused their stock to jump when they announced the product. Today, there are more Model I's than any other computer, the software base is enormous, and the Model I even commands its own national magazine called '80 Microcomputing!

SINCLAIR ZX-80

Name and Model Number Sinclair ZX-80.

Manufacturer's Name and Address Sinclair Research Ltd., 475 Main Street, PO Box 3027, Wallingford, CT 06492.

Architecture Pseudo-handheld, book-size unit requires external television for display. Uses Z-80 microprocessor.

Maximum RAM Memory Capacity 1K bytes (16K coming).

Mass Storage Device With Base Unit External cassette recorder (not supplied).

Price with Base RAM $199.95 (1K) plus $5.00 shipping (mail order only).

SINCLAIR ZX-80
(Continued)

Price with Maximum RAM

Not applicable.

Display Type

Black and white television, rf modulator built-in.

Screen Format

Text: 32 columns by 24 lines with 20 graphics characters on a 4 by 4 matrix. CHR$ and PRINT statements used to display and control graphics.

Number of Colors

None.

Sound Capability

None.

Expandability

8K floating point BASIC and 16K RAM planned.

Software Media

Cassette tape.

Special Features

Compact touch sensitive keyboard, one key command typing, access to 60 Hz clock.

Comments

Another marvel in miniaturization from Sinclair Ltd., a maker of miniature televisions and calculators. Only 12 ounces and 6½ by 8½ by 1½ inches. Sold only through the mail, the ZX-80 uses a Z-80 microprocessor and is a best seller in Europe. Only short programs allowed in 1K RAM. Clive Sinclair has big plans for the ZX-80. 30-day money back guarantee.

TEXAS INSTRUMENTS TI-99/4

Name and Model Number	TI-99/4.
Manufacturer's Name and Address	Texas Instruments Inc., PO Box 1444, Houston, TX 77001.
Architecture	Desktop color unit with 16-bit TI 9900 microprocessor.
Maximum RAM Memory Capacity	16K bytes.
Mass Storage Device With Base Unit	Dual cassette interface (recorder not included).
Price with Base RAM	$950 (16K).

TEXAS INSTRUMENTS TI-99/4
(Continued)

Price with Maximum RAM Same as base price.

Display Type Requires either TI 13-inch color monitor ($450) or color television and TI's modulator ($75.00).

Screen Format Text: 32 columns by 24 lines. Graphics 32h by 24v elements. Though a low resolution, each graphics character is an 8 by 8 cell which you can alter from BASIC. Up to 256h by 192v high resolution when TI provides machine language programming information.

Number of Colors 15 colors.

Sound Capability Three independent sound oscillators for 3 note chords with 5 octave range.

Expandability Dual mini-disk drives, printer, modem, and speech synthesizer. No bus.

Software Media Single slot for solid-state software cartridges, cassette and floppy diskette.

Special Features Speech synthesizer allows the 99/4 to speak over 300 words, programs are available which use it and you can add speech to your BASIC programs.

TEXAS INSTRUMENTS TI-99/4
(Continued)

Comments
The 99/4 is a most advanced personal computer in terms of its peripheral devices. The speech synthesizer allows incredible games and teaching programs. However, the avid hacker is presently locked out from using the TI's 16-bit microprocessor. An especially good computer for its complement of teaching programs for children 3 to 6 years of age.

VECTOR GRAPHICS SYSTEM B

Name and Model Number

Vector Graphics System B.

Manufacturer's Name and Address

Vector Graphics, 31364 Via Colinas, Westlake Village, CA 91361.

Architecture

S-100 mainframe using Z-80 microprocessor board.

Maximum RAM Memory Capacity

56K bytes.

Mass Storage Device With Base Unit

Two quad density mini-floppy disk drives in separate cabinet for 630K bytes on line mass storage.

VECTOR GRAPHICS SYSTEM B
(Continued)

Price with Base RAM

$5463 (56K CP/M 2 included).

Price with Maximum RAM

Same.

Display Type

Memory mapped video board drives supplied crt terminal.

Screen Format

Text: 64 columns by 16 lines, upper-case and lower-case on 7 by 9 dot matrix. Graphics: 128 horizontal elements by 48 vertical elements. 80 by 24 board Flashwriter II available as is high resolution 256h by 240v graphics board.

Number of Colors

None.

Sound Capability

None.

Expandability

Three S-100 slots provided, additional 18-slot motherboard available.

Software Media

Mini-floppy diskettes.

Special Features

Uses video board to run what looks like a serial terminal (parallel cable runs to terminal) for faster screen update than is possible with a serial terminal).

Comments

Very popular among business and professional users.

ZENITH DATA SYSTEMS Z-89F

Name and Model Number	Zenith Data Systems Z-89F.
Manufacturer's Name and Address	Zenith Data Systems, Hilltop Road, St. Joseph, MI 49085.
Architecture	Desktop with built-in crt monitor. Uses two Z-80 microprocessors.
Maximum RAM Memory Capacity	48K bytes.
Mass Storage Device With Base Unit	Built-in single density mini-floppy disk drive (100K byte capacity), cassette tape interface.
Price with Base RAM	$2595 (16K).

ZENITH DATA SYSTEM Z-89F
(Continued)

Price with Maximum RAM	$2895 (48K).
Display Type	Built-in 12-inch high resolution black and white crt.
Screen Format	Text: 80 columns by 24 lines, 5 by 7 dot matrix upper-case, 5 by 9 for lower-case with descenders. Special 25th line nonscrolling status line. Graphics: 33 built-in graphics characters on an 8 by 10 dot matrix accessible via BASIC PRINT and CHR$ commands.
Number of Colors	Not applicable.
Sound Capability	None.
Expandability	Two serial ports, no bus output or expansion, but disk expansion.
Software Media	Mini disk, cassette.
Special Features	High quality crt with P4 phosphor, numeric keypad, two Z-80s allow terminal and computer to run independently. Extra 16K of RAM is $150.
Comments	This is an assembled Heathkit H-89, sold through the parent company of Heath. A very nicely designed computer and second to the PET to go totally integrated (crt+keyboard +disk in one box). Zenith provides CP/M and all the assembled Heath peripherals. See Heathkit H-89.

CHAPTER 7

Getting Started

In this chapter we will find out how one goes about getting started in personal computing. You can approach your involvement with computers from several directions, some of which may even increase your earning power as you learn to use the computer. We will see how computers are becoming cheaper, easier to use, and more powerful. Finally, we will discover how to get a computer for free.

EDUCATING YOURSELF

Like any hobby, personal computing requires a certain awareness of computer subjects. It does not mean PhD-level understanding, just a simplified knowledge of certain concepts, and a feeling for some of the types of problems you may encounter in using a computer. You will want to discover right away what today's computers can do. You will also want to see a personal computer in action.

Become Aware of Computers

Start your journey to computer land by visiting a computer store. There are hundreds now, and thousands to come. The telephone companies are already making a special heading, "Computer Stores," in the Yellow Pages. At a computer store you can sit down and personally experience one of many different computer systems. You can play computer chess, or Star Trek, or many other interactive games. You can look at the various items offered for sale. Usually the magazines of small computing are offered, as are books and learning materials on microcomputers. Ask for a demonstration. Get an employee to tell you his personal reasons for using a computer. Find out what these devices are capable of doing. Finally ask for the names of some local computer clubs, and take the next step.

Visit a Computer Club

Perhaps the quickest way to get started in computing is to find a group of people with similar interests. There will always be someone who knows something you do not. Computer people love to trade information. In fact one of the most interesting aspects of computing is its gossip. There are clubs springing up constantly, and there is probably one within 25 miles of where you live.

Clubs offer all kinds of formats, with lectures, clinics, demonstrations, product previews, show and tell sessions, workshops, panel discussions, and tape slide programs. Some clubs have a

Become aware—visit a computer store.

"random access" period where everyone has a chance to make an announcement.

Before you go to a club, think about what you want to do with a computer. Plan out how it might work and why you think that it is important. Bring this information with you to share with others; or find some special aspect of a project to master, then see if anyone can use your energy. Whatever you do, don't just stand around and look.

Go to a Convention or a Computer Fair

Another growing phenomena among computer hobbyists are the so-called Computer Faires (sic), conferences, expositions, and conventions. These are highly charged, dynamic events; often hundreds of companies display their products, present lectures, award prizes, hold drawings, show movies, have special contests for the best computer, etc. You can collect an incredible array of literature for free. Sometimes you can even cajole someone into giving you a manual. If you are thinking about how to get the money to buy your first computer, then first try a smaller investment—reading.

Read, Read, Read

In order to ask intelligent questions you need to gather some basic information on your own. The fastest and cheapest way to get acquainted with a hobby is to read magazines and books on the subject. The magazines on personal computing have grown rapidly in number and more are certainly on the way. The magazines claim personal computering will be *the* biggest hobby, because it includes all other hobbies! Their pages contain articles on every imaginable aspect of home computing. Computer magazines offer insights into the future, and are proving grounds for different ways to disseminate information (one magazine is now publishing certain articles in what is called "machine readable format"). This allows your computer to read the information from the magazine page and put it directly into its memory.

Our suggestion is to purchase, or borrow, at least one issue of all the magazines, and use the "reader service" postcards in the magazine to send for advertisers' literature. All you have to do is circle numbers on the card which correspond to the numbers under each ad. This literature will provide you with hours of interesting and low-cost reading, and be an educational experience as well.

Exchange ideas—visit a computer club.

Some of the more popular of these magazines include:

Byte
Creative Computing
Doctor Dobbs Journal of Computer Calisthenics and Orthodontia
Interface
Interface Age
Kilobaud
Personal Computing

You can find these magazines at some newsstands (especially around heavy technological areas), libraries, and schools; or you can write to the magazines and ask for a sample issue. Get their addresses at your library.

Are You in the Deep or on the Surface?

There are basically two general types of personal computer users. One, which we'll call the "typical user," is simply concerned with getting the computer doing something, like figuring their income tax, or playing neat games of skill. The other type, which we'll call the "hobbyist," is concerned with many aspects of computers. The hobbyist enjoys programming languages, electronic

Discover new products—visit a convention.

circuits, and, in general, the "technical" side of computers. Since the needs of these two groups of personal computer users are so different, and the market is still changing, let's examine both levels of computer involvement.

If you are a hobbyist then you are probably "in the deep," and plan on making computers your profession. In this case your path involves a serious learning commitment. You will have to study basic electricity, chips, logic, computer math, programming, and computer systems. You may plan to become a consultant in the personal computing field, in which case you will really have to know your stuff. Or you may just enjoy creating new applications for computers. The hobbyist will consider building his own computer from a kit, and constructing special peripheral circuits for it.

If you are a typical user then you are more interested in what the computer is doing, than in how it does it. In your case the company that sells the computer will provide you with all the parts and accessories to do what you want. You may have to get a programmer consultant from outside the company if you want to do

Read to learn—literature saves time and money.

something special, but the manufacturer will supply all the hardware.

The basic difference between these two groups is that the hobbyist has a much greater flexibility of computer applications. He can single-handedly take on extremely sophisticated applications and probably get them working in short order. The typical user, on the other hand, can only choose from what the manufacturer has to offer. Because of these differences, companies recognize hobbyists as the pioneers of personal computing. Manufacturers watch this group carefully to get new ideas for creative computer products for the typical user group.

The typical user of computers will probably need to learn very little about how they work. But just as a stereo owner needs to know how to operate the volume and tone controls, so the personal computer owner will at least have to know how to use a keyboard. (This doesn't mean, however, that you have to know how to type. You may only be entering numbers.)

If you are interested in really "getting deep" into computers in a big way, then why not start your education right here. You now know enough to walk into any computer store and not be shocked out of your wits. The next logical step is to pick up a few books and see if your interest is still aroused. Write the various book publisers and ask for their catalog of current offerings and prices. Also, the magazines listed previously will have advertisements of books related to the computer field.

BUYING A COMPUTER

Ten years ago anyone reading this heading would have laughed. "Buy a computer? Got $100,000?" But buying a personal computer will soon be as commonplace as buying a calculator. You will walk into a major department store, try out the various computers, ask the salesperson questions, and probably walk out with the last decade's equivalent of a million dollars in computer equipment. Given the rapid changes in computer technology, the personal computer will hang over your shoulder in a carrying case, and in a few years will shrink to the size of a small camera.

Until that time, however, buying a personal computer may be a tricky job. Much will depend on just what you want the computer to do. If, for example, you just want something to keep the kids occupied, which is also educational, you may go out and spend $50 to $200 on a computerized tv game. But if you want to control the electrical consumption in your home, run the air conditioning system, and calculate your income tax, things may be quite a bit different. A hobbyist would have no problem here, but the typical user will have to wait until some company sells the entire application, or learn to be a hobbyist.

A resourceful person would be wise to just study computers for a while. Given the volatile changes taking place in the computer marketplace, the concept of waiting (as many people learned with calculators), may prove to be quite an advantage. Computers will definitely drop in price, although not as dramatically as the pocket calculator. One can certainly envision all kinds of products calling themselves computers, like "smart" appliances, microwave ovens, intelligent games, etc., and this will make things seem even more complicated. But, the proverb "know what you want to do" holds. Don't consider a smart tv game a computer if all you want to do is regulate your electricity.

FREE COMPUTERS

Everyone knows you can't get something for nothing. At least that is what the old proverb says. But computers are an exception.

Buying your personal computer is exciting.

Given a good imagination, and a powerful microcomputer, an average high school student can start a business and have the computer pay for itself.

Today low-cost microcomputers are making unique business ventures possible. Services such as mailing label preparation, manuscript word processing and editing, classified newspapers, and general data processing can be based around a personal computer. Computer dating, club organization, family budget planning, nutrition analyzing, even weight reduction can be centered around a good computer.

The trick to getting a computer for free is figuring out how to

194

get it to produce income. Perhaps you can write programs on it and sell them to magazines or companies. Perhaps you can develop a unique peripheral for your computer and sell it in the hobbyist marketplace. Or maybe you can develop a special application on your computer such as solar heating or energy regulation for the home, and then interest a manufacturer in buying it outright. Whatever you do, don't limit your imagination. One computer hobbyist sold his computer application to a farmer; it weighed chickens and saved him $2000 per month in overweight packages!

Numbering Systems

"What's one and one and one and one and one and one and one and one and one and one?"
"I don't know," said Alice. "I lost count."
"She can't do addition," said the Red Queen.
(Lewis Carroll, *Through the Looking Glass*)

No one knows when the first number was recorded, but most likely it dates back to Biblical times. Among the oldest system of numbers was that of the Chinese, which was first based on a system of laying sticks in patterns and later was based on symbols drawn with pen and ink.

Calculating in these number systems was exceedingly difficult. This was because each time the basic numerals were exceeded, a new numeral had to be invented. In Roman numerals, when you needed to count above 100, you used a *C*, and above 1000 an *M*. The real problem came when these numbers had to be multiplied. The actual process of counting took place on counting boards, such as the Chinese abacus, where answers were converted back to the notation system.

Our current decimal system is much more streamlined than those of the ancient civilizations. We only have to learn the 10 basic symbols and the positional notation system in order to count to any number. For example, what is the meaning of the number 256? In positional notation, the value of each digit is determined by its position. The four in 4000 has a different value than the 4 in

400. Thus, in 256 we have three digits, and each must be "interpreted" in light of where it is in order and relation to the other digits. We learn that the rightmost digit is interpreted as the number of "ones," the next to the left as the number of "tens," and the next digit as "hundreds." The general formula for representing numbers in the decimal system using positional notation is:

$$a_1 10^{n-1} + a_2 10^{n-2} + \ldots + a_n$$

which is expressed as $a_1 a_2 a_3 \ldots a_n$, where n is the number of digits to the left of the decimal point. Therefore,

$$256 = (2 \times 10^2) + (5 \times 10^1) + (6 \times 10^0)$$
$$= 2 \text{ hundreds} + 5 \text{ tens} + 6 \text{ ones}$$

In the decimal system we use 10 as the basic multiplier. We call 10 the *base* or *radix*. Most of recorded history shows mankind counting in the decimal system (base 10). However, it is not difficult to imagine a race of one-armed people who used the quinary system (base 5). We see examples of the duodecimal system in clocks, rulers, the dozen, and so on.

THE BINARY SYSTEM

Although the seventeenth-century German mathematician Leibnitz was given most of the credit for invention of the binary number system with a base of 2, it was probably the ancient Chinese who realized the simple and natural way of representing numbers as powers of 2.

Early computers used relays and switches as their basic elements. The operation of a switch or a relay is itself binary in nature. A switch can either be on (1) or off (0). Modern computers use transistors like those found in televisions and radios. These components can be arranged to be in one or two "states": on or off. As a matter of fact, the more distinctly different the two states, the more reliable the computer's operation.

The idea is to make the devices work in such a manner that even slight changes in their characteristics will not affect the operation. The best way of doing this is to use a *bistable device*, which has two states.

If a bistable device is in stable state X, an energy pulse will drive it to state Y; and if the bistable component is in stable state

(A) Chinese "stick" number system.

1 2 3 4 5 6 7 8 9

1 2 3 4 5

6 7 8 9 10

(B) Chinese "pen-and-ink" number system.

First number systems.

Y, an energy pulse will drive it to state X. It is easy for a bistable component to represent the number 0 or 1:

$$\text{stable state } X = 1$$
$$\text{stable state } Y = 0$$

Counting

The same type of positional notation used in the decimal system is used in the binary. Since there are only two possible states for a numeral, either we count the position value or we don't count it. The general rule is: The binary number $a_1a_2a_3 \ldots a_n$ is expressed in decimal as:

$$a_1 2^{n-1} + a_2 2^{n-2} + \ldots + a_n$$

Therefore, the binary number 11010 is converted to decimal as follows:

$$N = a_1 2^{5-1} + a_2 2^{4-1} + a_3 2^{3-1} + a_4 2^{2-1} + a_5 2^{1-1}$$
$$= a_1 16 + a_2 8 + a_3 4 + a_4 2 + a_5 1$$

Substituting the values for a_1, a_2, a_3, a_4, and a_5:

$$11010 = (1 \times 16) + (1 \times 8) + (0 \times 4) + (1 \times 2) + (0 \times 1)$$
$$= 16 + 8 + 0 + 2 + 0$$
$$= 26 \text{ (decimal system)}$$

The first 20 binary numbers are listed below.

The First 20 Binary Numbers

Decimal	Binary	Decimal	Binary
1	1	11	1011
2	10	12	1100
3	11	13	1101
4	100	14	1110
5	101	15	1111
6	110	16	10000
7	111	17	10001
8	1000	18	10010
9	1001	19	10011
10	1010	20	10100

A simpler way to convert binary numbers to decimal is to use a weighting table. This is simply a reduction of the expansion formula just presented. Write down the value of the positions in the binary number over the binary digits, arrange them as an addition, and add them.

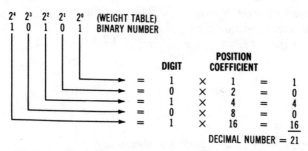

Binary-to-decimal conversion using the weighting method.

Frequently we will want to convert in the opposite direction, from decimal to binary. For this method we repeatedly divide the decimal number by 2, and the remainder after each division is used to indicate the coefficients of the binary number to be formed. The figure below shows the conversion of 47_{10} to binary. Note that decimal 47 is written 47_{10} and that binary numbers are given the subscript 2 if there is danger of confusing the number systems.

Fractional numbers are treated in the same manner as in the decimal system. In the decimal system:

$$0.128 = (1 \times 10^{-1}) + (2 \times 10^{-2}) + (8 \times 10^{-3})$$

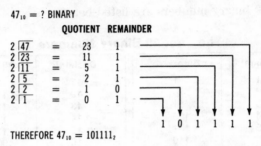

THEREFORE $47_{10} = 101111_2$

Decimal-to-binary conversion using the division method.

In the binary system:

$$0.101 = (1 \times 2^{-1}) + (0 \times 2^{-2}) + (1 \times 2^{-3})$$

Binary Addition and Subtraction

Addition in binary is as easy as addition in decimal, and follows the same rules. In adding decimal $1 + 8$, we get a sum of 9. This is the highest-value digit. Adding 1 to 9 requires that we change the digit back to 0 *and carry 1*. Similarly, adding binary $0 + 1$, we reach the highest-value binary digit, 1. Adding 1 to 1 requires that we change the 1 back to a 0 and carry 1, i.e., $1 + 1 = 10$. Thus, for example, add binary 101 to 111:

$$101_2 = 5_{10}$$
$$+ \ 111_2 = 7_{10}$$
$$1100_2 = 12_{10}$$

The four rules of binary addition are:

$$0 + 0 = 0$$
$$0 + 1 = 1$$
$$1 + 0 = 1$$
$$1 + 1 = 0, \text{ carry } 1$$

Here are some examples:

101	5	11.01	3¼
+ 110	6	101.11	5¾
1011	11	1001.00	9

Subtraction is just inverted addition. It is necessary to establish a convention for subtracting a large digit from a small digit. This condition occurs in binary math when we subtract a 1 from a 0. The remainder is 1, and we borrow 1 from the column to the left. Just as in decimal subtraction, if the digit on the left is a 1, we make it a zero, and if it's a zero, we make it a 1. The rules for binary subtraction are:

$$0 - 0 = 0$$
$$1 - 0 = 1$$
$$1 - 1 = 0$$
$$0 - 1 = 1, \text{ borrow } 1$$

Here are two examples:

10000	16	110.01	6¼
− 11	− 3	−100.1	−4½
1101	13	1.11	1¾

Binary Multiplication and Division

There are only four basic multiplications to remember in the binary system, instead of the usual 100 we memorize in the decimal system. The binary multiplication table is:

$$0 \times 0 = 0$$
$$1 \times 0 = 0$$
$$0 \times 1 = 0$$
$$1 \times 1 = 1$$

The following examples illustrate how easy binary multiplication is compared with decimal. The rule to remember is: "copy the multiplicand if the multiplier is a 1, and copy all 0's if the multiplier is a 0. Then add down, as in decimal multiplication."

Binary	Decimal	Binary	Decimal
1100	12	1.01	1.25
×1010	× 10	× 10.1	× 2.5
0000	120	101	625
1100		1010	250
0000		11.001	3.125
1100			
1111000			

Binary division is also very simple. Division by zero is forbidden, just as in decimal division. The binary division table is:

$$\frac{0}{1} = 0$$

$$\frac{1}{1} = 1$$

Examples of binary division are:

Binary	*Decimal*
101	5
101)11001	5)25
101	
101	
101	

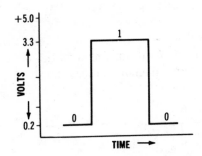

(A) Binary digit representation (TTL).

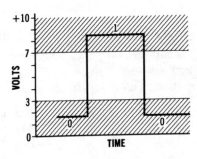

(B) Binary digit representation (CMOS).

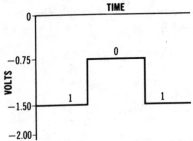

(C) Binary digit representation— negative logic (ECL).

Representing binary numbers.

Because of the difficult binary additions and subtractions that result when the numbers are large, octal or hexadecimal notation is often used.

Representing Binary Numbers

Information in digital computers of today is processed by the switching and storing of electrical signals. Computers operating in the binary number system need represent only one of two values (1 and 0) at a time. A single wire can be utilized for this purpose. A method for representing a binary digit on a signal line is shown in (A) of the figure. In this method a small positive voltage is used to represent a 0, and a larger positive dc voltage is used to represent a 1.

Much importance is placed on the actual voltage values used to represent the binary digit. Usually, the circuitry used to transmit and receive these signals determines the range of voltages. The most ideal circuit is one in which the two logic levels are far apart.

Note that the "1" signal is positive with respect to the "0" signal. This convention could also have been reversed, i.e., the negative-most signal called a "1" and the more positive signal a "0." Usually, one convention is chosen by the designer and then used throughout the computer.

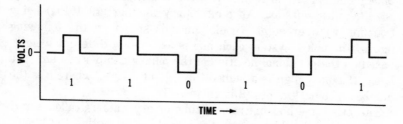

(A) RZ method of representing binary digits.

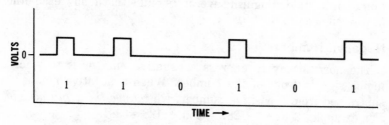

(B) NRZ method of representing binary digits.

Pulse representation of binary numbers.

Pulse Representation of Binary Numbers

Binary digits are often transmitted and received as a burst of pulses. A system in which a positive pulse represents a 1 and a negative pulse a 0 is shown in the figure. The signal line remains at some in-between value when no pulse is being sent. This technique is used frequently in magnetic recording, and is called *return-to-zero* (RZ) encoding.

A more popular technique is shown in (B) of the figure. A 1 is represented by a pulse, and a 0 as no pulse. The receive circuitry must keep in synchronization with the incoming signal in order to know when a binary digit is occurring. This technique is called *non-return-to-zero* (NRZ) encoding.

Serial and Parallel Transmission

So far, methods of representing and transmitting a single binary digit have been illustrated. We will find that it is often necessary to transmit complete binary numbers, which is accomplished by transmitting each binary digit over its own wire. Thus, an n-digit binary number would require n wires or signal lines. This is called *parallel transmission*. An 8-bit binary number (10010101) being transmitted over eight parallel lines is shown in the following figure. In such a system each line is assigned a different weight, based on the positional notation of the binary number system. The leftmost binary digit is assigned the weight of 2^{n-1}, where n is the number of binary digits (8 in this case).

The other method of transmitting binary data is called *serial transmission*. In this method the signals representing the binary digits are transmitted one at a time in sequence, usually starting with the rightmost digit. This method requires some synchronization in order to distinguish several 0's or 1's that follow each other in a sequence.

Negative Numbers

The normal way to express a negative number is to place a minus sign in front of the number. When a negative number is subtracted from a positive number, we *change the sign and add.* For example, $256 - (-128) = 256 + 128 = 384$.

Digital computers use binary storage devices to store and represent binary digits. Seven such devices can represent the binary numbers from 0000000 to 1111111 (0 to 127_{10}). However, if we wish

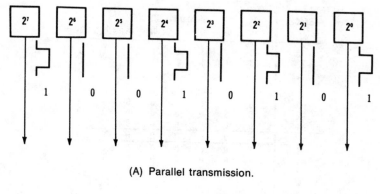

(A) Parallel transmission.

(B) Serial transmission.

Parallel and serial transmission.

to increase the range to include the negative numbers from 0000000 to −1111111, we need another binary digit, or bit. This bit is called the *sign bit* and is placed in front of the most significant digit of the binary number.

The convention for the sign bit is: If the sign bit is 0, the number is positive; and if the sign bit is a 1, the number is negative. The remaining digits form the absolute value of the number. This numerical storage mode is called *signed binary*.

Signed binary, although frequently used, has a few minor flaws that make it less flexible than other codes for negative numbers. Any arithmetic operation requires checking the sign bit and then either adding or subtracting the numerical values, based on the signs.

The Use of Complements

The use of complemented binary numbers makes it possible to add or subtract binary numbers using only circuitry for addition. To see how negative numbers are used in the computer, consider a mechanical register, such as a car mileage indicator, being rotated

INTEGER	SIGNED BINARY CODE							
	s	b_7	b_6	b_5	b_4	b_3	b_2	b_1
+127	0	1	1	1	1	1	1	1
+126	0	1	1	1	1	1	1	0
⋮				⋮				
+3	0	0	0	0	0	0	1	1
+2	0	0	0	0	0	0	1	0
+1	0	0	0	0	0	0	0	1
0	0	0	0	0	0	0	0	0
−1	1	0	0	0	0	0	0	1
−2	1	0	0	0	0	0	1	0
−3	1	0	0	0	0	0	1	1
⋮				⋮				
−126	1	1	1	1	1	1	1	0
−127	1	1	1	1	1	1	1	1

(A) Seven-bit-magnitude table.

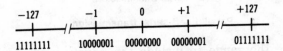

(B) Signed binary number line (seven-bit magnitude).

Signed binary code.

backwards. A five-digit register approaching and passing through zero would read as follows:

$$00005$$
$$00004$$
$$00003$$
$$00002$$
$$00001$$
$$00000$$
$$99999$$
$$99998$$
$$99997$$
$$\text{etc.}$$

It should be clear that the number 99998 corresponds to −2. Furthermore, if we add

$$00005$$
$$+ \ 99998$$
$$\overline{1 \quad 00003}$$

and ignore the carry to the left, we have effectively formed the operation of subtraction: $5 - 2 = 3$.

The number 99998 is called the *ten's complement* of 2. The ten's complement of any decimal number may be formed by subtracting each digit of the number from 9, and then adding 1 to the least significant digit of the number formed. For example:

normal
subtraction

$$89$$
$$- \ 23$$
$$\overline{66}$$

ten's complement
subtraction

$$89 \qquad 89$$
$$- \ 23 \qquad + \ 77$$
$$\longrightarrow 1 \quad 66$$

└─ DROP CARRY

Two's Complement

The two's complement is the binary equivalent of the ten's complement in the decimal system. It is defined as that number which, when added to the original number, will result in a sum of zero, ignoring the carry. The following example points this out:

$$1101 \quad \text{number}$$
$$\underline{0011} \quad \text{two's complement}$$
$$\longrightarrow 1 \ 0000 \quad \text{sum}$$

└─ IGNORE CARRY

The easiest method of finding the two's complement of a binary number is to first find the one's complement, which is formed by setting each bit to the opposite value:

$$11011101 \quad \text{number}$$
$$00100010 \quad \text{one's complement}$$

The two's complement of the number is then obtained by adding 1 to the least significant digit of the one's complement:

$$11011101 \quad \text{number}$$
$$00100010 \quad \text{one's complement}$$
$$\underline{+1} \quad \text{add one}$$
$$00100011 \quad \text{two's complement}$$

The complete signed two's complement code is obtained for negative numbers by using a 1 for the sign bit, and two's complement for the magnitude of the number.

In contrast to the signed binary code, in the signed two's complement code, numbers can be added without regard to their signs and the result will always be correct. The following examples should make this clear:

$$
\begin{array}{rr}
0000101 & 5 \\
+1111110 & +\ (-2) \\
\hline
\rightarrow\!1\ \ 0000011 & 3 \\
\text{IGNORE}
\end{array}
\qquad
\begin{array}{rr}
1111011 & -5 \\
+0000010 & +\ (+2) \\
\hline
11111101 & (-3) \\
\end{array}
\qquad
\begin{array}{rr}
1111011 & -5 \\
+1111110 & +\ (-2) \\
\hline
\rightarrow\!1\ \ 1111001 & (-7) \\
\text{IGNORE}
\end{array}
$$

INTEGER	SIGNED 2's COMPLEMENT CODE							
	s	b_7	b_6	b_5	b_4	b_3	b_2	b_1
+127	0	1	1	1	1	1	1	1
+126	0	1	1	1	1	1	1	0
⋮				⋮				
+3	0	0	0	0	0	0	1	1
+2	0	0	0	0	0	0	1	0
+1	0	0	0	0	0	0	0	1
0	0	0	0	0	0	0	0	0
−1	1	1	1	1	1	1	1	1
−2	1	1	1	1	1	1	1	0
−3	1	1	1	1	1	1	0	1
⋮				⋮				
−126	1	0	0	0	0	0	1	0
−127	1	0	0	0	0	0	0	1
−128	1	0	0	0	0	0	0	0

(A) Seven-bit-magnitude table.

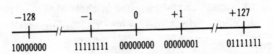

(B) Two's complement number line.

Signed two's complement code.

Notice that it is impossible to add $+64$ to $+64$ in a 7-bit code and $+128$ to $+128$ in an 8-bit code. Also note that in comparing the two systems, signed binary and two's complement, the largest negative two's complement number that can be represented in 8 bits is -128, while in signed binary it's -127. Changing a negative integer from signed binary to two's complement requires simply complementing all bits except the sign bit, and adding 1.

Binary-Coded Number Representation

Since computers operate in the binary number system, while people use the decimal system, it was only natural that some intermediate system be developed. Computers, and some calculators and "intelligent" instruments, use a *binary-coded decimal* system. In such systems, a group of binary bits is used to represent each of the 10 decimal digits.

The binary-coded decimal (bcd) system is called a "weighted binary code" with the weights 8, 4, 2, and 1, as shown in the table. Notice that 4 binary bits are required for each decimal digit, and that each digit is assigned a weight: the leftmost bit has a weight of 8; the rightmost bit a weight of 1.

There's a slight problem with using 4 bits to represent 10 decimal values. Since $2^4 = 16$, the 4 bits could actually represent 16 values. However, the next choice down, 3 bits, allows only 2^3, or 8, possible digits, which is insufficient. To represent the decimal number 127 in bcd, 12 binary bits are required instead of seven if we use pure binary:

$$
\begin{array}{ccc}
1 & 2 & 7 \\
0001 & 0010 & 0111
\end{array}
$$

The bcd system has another property that makes it less flexible for binary computation in the computer. The difficulty lies in forming complements of its numbers. As was pointed out, it is common practice to perform subtraction by complementing the subtrahend and adding 1. When the bcd 8-4-2-1 system is used, the complement formed by inverting all the bits may produce an illegal bcd digit. For example, complementing the bcd number 0010 (2_{10}) gives 1101 (13_{10}), which is not a bcd code.

To solve this problem, several other codes have been developed. For example, the *excess-three code* is formed by adding 3 to the decimal number and then forming the bcd code. For example:

$$\begin{array}{r} 4 \\ +3 \\ \hline 7 \end{array} \quad \begin{array}{l} \text{number} \\ \text{add for excess-three} \\ \\ \end{array}$$

$$7 = 0111 \quad \text{convert 7 to bcd}$$

The excess-three codes for the 10 decimal digits are shown. Now the complement of the excess-three code doesn't form any illegal bcd digits, i.e., 10_{10} or above.

Binary-Coded Number Representation

Decimal Digit	Binary-Coded Decimal	Excess-3 Coded Binary	2-4-2-1 Coded Binary Weight of Bit			
			2	4	2	1
0	0000	0011	0	0	0	0
1	0001	0100	0	0	0	1
2	0010	0101	0	0	1	0
3	0011	0110	0	0	1	1
4	0100	0111	0	1	0	0
5	0101	1000	1	0	1	1
6	0110	1001	1	1	0	0
7	0111	1010	1	1	0	1
8	1000	1011	1	1	1	0
9	1001	1100	1	1	1	1

The excess-three code is not a weighted code, since the sum of the bits does not equal the number being represented. On the other hand, the bcd 8-4-2-1 code is weighted but forms illegal complements.

A weighted code that does form legal complements is the *2-4-2-1 code* in the table.

OCTAL NUMBER SYSTEM

It is probably quite evident by now that the binary number system, although nice for computers, is a little cumbersome for human usage. For example, communicating binary 11011010 over a telephone would be "one-one-zero-one-one-zero-one-zero," which is quite a mouthful. Also, it is easy to make errors when adding and subtracting large binary numbers. The octal (base 8) number system alleviates most of these problems and is frequently used in the microcomputer literature.

The octal system uses the digits 0 through 7 in forming numbers. Octal numbers and their decimal equivalents are shown below.

First 13 Octal Digits

Decimal	Octal	Binary	Decimal	Octal	Binary
0	0	0	7	7	111
1	1	1	8	10	1000
2	2	10	9	11	1001
3	3	11	10	12	1010
4	4	100	11	13	1011
5	5	101	12	14	1100
6	6	110	13	15	1101

Octal numbers are converted to decimal numbers by using the same expansion formula as that used in binary-to-decimal conversion, except that 8 is used for the base instead of 2.

$$
\begin{aligned}
\text{(octal) } 167 &= (1 \times 8^2) + (6 \times 8^1) + (7 \times 8^0) \\
&= (1 \times 64) + (6 \times 8) + (7 \times 1) \\
&= \quad 64 \quad + \quad 48 \quad + \quad 7 \\
&= 119 \text{ (decimal)}
\end{aligned}
$$

A *weighting table* is a quick way to convert octal values to decimal.

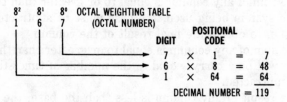

Octal-to-decimal conversion.

The primary use of octal is as a convenient way of recording values stored in binary registers. This is accomplished by using a grouping method to convert the binary value to its octal equivalent. The binary number is grouped by threes, starting with the bit corresponding to $2^0 = 1$ and grouping to the left of it. Then each binary group is converted to its octal equivalent. For example, convert 11110101 to octal:

```
 ┌→011   110   101   binary number
 │    3    6    5    octal equivalent
 └── implied 0
```

The largest 8-bit octal number is 377_8, and the largest 7-bit octal number is 177_8. Negative octal numbers in 8-bit signed two's complement cover 377_8 (-1_{10}) to 200_8 (-128_{10}).

Conversion from decimal to octal is performed by repeated division by 8 and using the remainder as a digit in the octal number being formed.

$1376_{10} = ?$ OCTAL

```
                    QUOTIENT   REMAINDER
        8 ⌐1376⌐       172         0
        8 ⌐ 172        21          4
        8 ⌐ 21          2          5
        8 ⌐ 2           0          2

                                       2   5   4   0
```

THEREFORE $136_{10} = 2540_8$

Decimal-to-octal conversion.

Addition in Octal

Octal addition is easy if we remember the following rules (which we will find also apply to hexadecimal):

1. If the sum of any column is equal to or greater than the base of the system being used, the base must be subtracted from the sum to obtain the final result of the column.
2. If the sum of any column is equal to or greater than the base, there will be a carry, equal to the number of times the base was subtracted.
3. If the result of any column is less than the base, the base is not subtracted and no carry will be generated.

Examples:

```
octal    decimal              octal     decimal
    5   = 5                        35  =    29
  +3   = 3                       +63  =  +51
  ───   ───                    ───────   ─────
    8                          1  10  8
  -8                            -8 -8
  ───                          ──────────
   10   = 8                    1  2  0  =    80
```

Octal Subtraction

Octal subtraction can be performed directly or in the complemented mode by using addition. In direct subtraction, whenever a borrow is needed, an 8 is borrowed and added to the number. For example:

$$2022_8 - 1234_8 = ?$$

$$\begin{array}{r} 2022_8 \\ 1234_8 \\ \hline 566_8 \end{array}$$

Octal subtraction may also be performed by finding the eight's complement and adding. The eight's complement is found by adding 1 to the seven's complement. The seven's complement of the number may be found by subtracting each digit from 7. For example:

$$377_8 - 261_8 = ?$$

a)
$$\begin{array}{rl} 777 & \\ -261 & \text{(second number)} \\ \hline 516 & \text{7's complement} \\ +1 & \\ \hline 517 & \text{8's complement} \end{array}$$

b)
$$\begin{array}{rl} 377 & \text{(first number)} \\ +517 & \text{8's complement of 261} \\ \hline \end{array}$$

$$\begin{array}{rrr} 9 & 9 & 14 \\ -8 & -8 & -8 \\ \hline 1 & 1 & 6 \end{array} = 116_8$$

Octal Multiplication

Octal multiplication is performed by using an octal multiplication table in the same manner as a decimal table would be used. All additions are done by using the rules for octal addition. For example:

$$17_8 \times 6_8 = ?$$ $$177_8 \times 27_8 = ?$$

octal			decimal	octal			decimal
	17	=	15		177	=	127
	×6	=	×6		×27	=	×23
1	11	2	90		1371		381
−0	−8	−0			376		254
1	3	2=132_8		5	11	13 1	2921
				−0	−8	−8 −0	
				5	3	5 1=5351_8	

Numbers are multiplied by looking up the result in the table. The result of any product larger than 7 (the radix or base) is carried and then octally added to the next product. The results are then summed up by using octal addition.

Octal Multiplication Table

×	0	1	2	3	4	5	6	7
0	0	0	0	0	0	0	0	0
1	0	1	2	3	4	5	6	7
2	0	2	4	6	10	12	14	16
3	0	3	6	11	14	17	22	25
4	0	4	10	14	20	24	30	34
5	0	5	12	17	24	31	36	43
6	0	6	14	22	30	36	44	52
7	0	7	16	25	34	43	52	61

Octal Division

Octal division uses the same principles as decimal division. All multiplication and subtraction involved, however, must be done in octal. Refer to the octal multiplication table. Some examples:

$$144_8 \div 2_8 = ?$$
$$\frac{144_8}{2_8} = \frac{100_{10}}{2_{10}} = 50_{10} = 62_8$$

$$62_8 \div 2_8 = ?$$ $$1714_8 \div 22_8 = ?$$

$$
\begin{array}{r}
31 = 31_8 = 25_{10} \\
2\overline{)62} \\
6 \\
\hline
02 \\
2 \\
\hline
0
\end{array}
$$

$$
\begin{array}{r}
66 = 66_8 = 54_{10} \\
22\overline{)1714} \\
154 \\
\hline
154 \\
154 \\
\hline
\end{array}
$$

THE HEXADECIMAL SYSTEM

Hexadecimal is another important and often-used computer number system. "Hex" uses the radix 16 and therefore has 16 digits. The first 10 digits are represented by the decimal digits 0 through 9, and the remaining six are indicated by the letters A, B, C, D, E, and F. There is nothing special about these letters, and any other letters could have been used. The first 16 hexadecimal digits are shown below.

First 16 Hexadecimal Digits

Binary	Hexadecimal	Decimal
0000	0	0
0001	1	1
0010	2	2
0011	3	3
0100	4	4
0101	5	5
0110	6	6
0111	7	7
1000	8	8
1001	9	9
1010	A	10
1011	B	11
1100	C	12
1101	D	13
1110	E	14
1111	F	15

Binary numbers are easily converted to hex by grouping the bits in groups of four, starting on the right, converting the results to decimal, and then converting to hex. For example:

$$1000 \ 1010 \ 1101 \ \text{binary}$$
$$8 \quad 10 \quad 13 \quad \text{decimal}$$
$$8 \quad A \quad D \quad \text{hex} = 8AD_{16}$$

As you can probably tell, hex is preferred over octal whenever the binary number to be represented is 16 bits or more. This is because the hex code is more compact than the octal equivalent.

Conversion from hexadecimal to decimal is straightforward but time-consuming. The expansion formula, or a weighting table with an intermediary hex-to-decimal conversion, is used as shown above.

$$975 = ?_{16}$$

	QUOTIENT	REMAINDER IN DECIMAL	REMAINDER IN HEX
975/16	60	15	F
60/16	3	12	C
3/16	0	3	3

3 C F

Hexadecimal-to-decimal conversion.

Conversion from decimal to hex is performed by repeatedly dividing the 16, and converting the remainder to a hex digit. The quotient becomes the next number to divide.

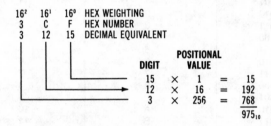

16^2	16^1	16^0	HEX WEIGHTING
3	C	F	HEX NUMBER
3	12	15	DECIMAL EQUIVALENT

DIGIT		POSITIONAL VALUE			
15	×	1	=	15
12	×	16	=	192
3	×	256	=	768
				975_{10}

Decimal-to-hexadecimal conversion.

Hexadecimal Addition

Addition in hex is similar to the addition procedure for octal, except the hex digits are first converted to decimal. For example:

$$3CF + 2AD = ?$$

+ 2AD =	+2	10	13
3CF =	3	12	15
	6	23	28
	−0−	16−	16
	6	7	12 = 67C

Subtraction in Hexadecimal

Subtraction in hex may be accomplished by either the direct or the complement method. In the direct method, the hex digits are converted to decimal. If a borrow is required, 16 is added to the desired number and the digit borrowed from is decreased by 1. In the complement method, the sixteen's complement of the subtrahend is determined and the two numbers are added. The sixteen's complement is found by adding 1 to the fifteen's complement. The fifteen's complement is found by subtracting each of the hex digits from F. For example:

$$2BD - 1CE = ?$$

FFF =	15	15	15	
−1CE	−1	12	14	second number
	14	3	1	15's complement
			+1	
	14	3	2	16's complement
2BD =	+2	11	13	first number
	1	16	14	15
	−16	−0	−0	
ignore carry	0	14	15	= EF (answer)

Hexadecimal Multiplication

Direct hex multiplication is rather tedious and time-consuming. This is because there are 256 entries in a hex multiplication table. The best method is to convert to decimal by using the expansion polynomial and then convert back from decimal to hex after computation.

Index

TO THE READER

Sams Computer books cover Fundamentals — Programming — Interfacing — Technology written to meet the needs of computer engineers, professionals, scientists, technicians, students, educators, business owners, personal computerists and home hobbyists.

*Our Tradition is to meet your needs
and in so doing we invite you to tell us what
your needs and interests are by completing
the following:*

1. I need books on the following topics:

_____

_____

_____

_____

_____

_____

2. I have the following Sams titles:

_____

_____

_____

_____

_____

_____

3. My occupation is:

_____ Scientist, Engineer	_____ D P Professional
_____ Personal computerist	_____ Business owner
_____ Technician, Serviceman	_____ Computer store owner
_____ Educator	_____ Home hobbyist
_____ Student	Other _____

Name (print) _____

Address _____

City _____ State _____ Zip _____

Mail to: **Howard W. Sams & Co., Inc.**
Marketing Dept. #CBS1/80
4300 W. 62nd St., P.O. Box 7092
Indianapolis, Indiana 46206

21860